St. Louis CARDINALS
YESTERDAY & TODAY ™

Bruce Herman
Foreword by Ozzie Smith
Rob Rains, Consultant

WEST
SIDE
PUBLISHING

Bruce Herman is a sportswriter, editor, and consultant based in Blacksburg, Virginia. Editorial consultant to The Topps Company since 1991, he has contributed to *Sports Illustrated* and many other major publications and has been internationally syndicated by Tribune Media. He writes regularly for Major League Baseball Publications and Athlon Sports and is the author of *Hall of Fame Players: Cooperstown*.

Ozzie Smith was elected to the Hall of Fame in his first year of eligibility after starring as the Cardinals' shortstop from 1982 to 1996. A 15-time All-Star, Smith won 13 Gold Gloves for his defensive excellence.

Rob Rains was the Cardinals beat writer for the *St. Louis Globe-Democrat* and has written numerous books about the team and its players, including co-authoring the autobiographies of Jack Buck, Red Schoendienst, and Ozzie Smith. He also co-hosts a baseball talk show on KMOX Radio in St. Louis.

Special thanks to collector **Ted Ingram,** to **SAD Memorabilia,** and to curator **Paula Homan** and registrar **Jennifer Jackson** of the St. Louis Cardinals Hall of Fame Museum.

Ted Ingram has been an avid St. Louis Cardinal fan all his life. His collection includes well over 2,000 items and more than 5,000 baseball cards dating back to the beginning of the team.

The **St. Louis Cardinals Hall of Fame Museum** is the official repository for the team, providing a collection of authentic and game-used memorabilia, as well as interpretive elements of photography, scorecards, programs, souvenirs, and all manner of materials relating to the full history of the National League team (1892–present).

Facts are verified by Dave Zeman.

Yesterday & Today is a trademark of West Side Publishing.

West Side Publishing is a division of Publications International, Ltd.

Louis Weber, CEO
Publications International, Ltd.
7373 North Cicero Avenue
Lincolnwood, Illinois 60712

ISBN-13: 978-1-4127-1504-1
ISBN-10: 1-4127-1504-0

Manufactured in China.

8 7 6 5 4 3 2 1

Library of Congress Control Number: 2007937673

Pages 14, 54, 68, 79, 86, 102, 114, 123, 132, 138: *St. Louis Post-Dispatch* clips reprinted with permission from the *St. Louis Post-Dispatch* © 1928, 1944, 1958, 1967, 1968, 1977, 1982, 1985, 1998, 2006.

Page 24: Excerpt from "H Is for Hornsby" © 1949 by Ogden Nash. Reprinted with permission from Curtis Brown, Ltd.

Page 60: *Parade Magazine* cover © 1956 by *Parade Magazine*. Reprinted with permission.

Page 78: *SPORT Magazine* cover image courtesy of thesportgallery.com. Copyright SPORT Gallery Inc.

Picture Credits

Front cover: Getty Images

Back cover: AP Images

Allied Photocolor: 64 (bottom), 67 (right); **AP Images:** contents, 49 (top left), 50 (bottom), 56 (bottom), 62 (bottom), 66, 85 (right), 90 (bottom), 99 (left), 101, 124 (bottom), 125, 126, 127 (top), 128 (left), 129, 131 (right), 134, 135 (top), 136 (left), 137 (top & bottom right), 142 (bottom); **Chicago History Museum:** *Chicago Daily News,* SDN-005710, 12 (bottom left), SDN-003412, 17 (left), SDN-069834, 20 (bottom), SDN-066151, 21; **Getty Images:** backgrounds, endsheets, 57 (bottom), 108 (right), 117 (top), 118 (top left), 119 (bottom right), 130, 135 (bottom); Diamond Images, 98 (right), 104 (left); Focus on Sport, contents, 72 (bottom), 75 (bottom), 80, 81 (right), 82, 85 (left), 88, 89 (top left & right center), 95, 105, 109, 110 (right), 111, 112, 113, 116 (bottom), 117 (bottom left), 118 (bottom), 120 (bottom right), 121 (right); George Gojkovich, 116 (top); MLB Photos, 7, 45 (left), 77 (bottom), 97, 119 (top); Ronald C. Modra/Sports Imagery, 121 (left); National Baseball Hall of Fame Library, contents; Herb Scharfman/Sports Imagery, 83 (top left & bottom), 84 (right), 140 (top); *Time Life* Pictures, 44 (right), 65 (left center, right center & far right); Transcendental Graphics, 9, 11 (bottom right), 43, 48 (bottom), 96 (left); **Ted Ingram Collection:** contents, 8 (bottom), 14 (left center & right center), 15 (top left), 18 (right), 20 (top), 26 (center & right), 27, 29 (left), 31 (left), 32 (left), 35 (right), 36 (top), 38, 39, 41 (right), 42 (right), 48 (top right), 49 (top right), 53 (left), 54, 55 (top right, bottom left & bottom right), 58 (left), 59 (bottom), 60, 61 (top left, top right & bottom), 64 (top), 68 (right), 69 (top left & bottom left), 70 (top), 71 (right), 72 (top left & top right), 76 (top), 78, 79 (right & center), 81 (left), 83 (top right), 84 (left), 86, 87, 89 (left center), 91 (bottom), 92, 93 (top left & right center), 98 (left), 100 (top), 102 (top right & bottom right), 103 (top left & bottom), 106 (top right), 107 (top left), 108 (left), 110 (left), 114 (right & bottom), 115 (top right & left center), 117 (bottom right), 122 (bottom left), 123 (top right & bottom), 124 (top), 127 (bottom), 128 (right), 131 (left), 132, 133 (top right & bottom), 135 (left center), 136 (right), 138 (top right), 139 (bottom left), 140 (bottom), 143 (top & bottom); *Sports Illustrated,* 74 (left); **Richard Johnson Collection:** 75 (top); **Library of Congress:** 10, 11 (top), 12 (top), 16 (left); **National Baseball Hall of Fame Library, Cooperstown, N.Y.:** 25, 29 (right), 31 (right), 32 (right), 33 (top & bottom), 36 (bottom), 37, 41 (bottom), 42 (left), 44 (bottom), 45 (top right & right center), 46 (bottom), 47, 48 (top left), 50 (top), 51 (left), 53 (right), 56 (top), 57 (top left), 58 (right), 63, 65 (far left), 70 (bottom), 74 (right), 76 (bottom), 77 (top), 90 (top); **PhotoDisc Collection:** sidebars; **PIL Collection:** contents, 16 (right), 22 (bottom), 23, 24 (left), 28, 30, 34, 35 (top), 40, 45 (center), 52, 59 (top), 91 (top), 100 (bottom), 107 (right); **SAD Memorabilia:** 44 (left), 61 (left center), 142 (top), 106 (top left), 133 (top left), 137 (bottom left); *Sports Illustrated,* 96 (right); **Courtesy of Ozzie Smith:** 6; **St. Louis Cardinals Hall of Fame Museum:** 3, contents, 8 (top), 13, 14 (top right), 15 (left center & right), 17 (right), 18 (left), 19, 22 (top), 24 (right), 26 (left), 46 (top), 51 (right), 55 (top left), 57 (top right), 62 (top), 67 (left), 68 (center), 69 (top right & bottom right), 71 (left), 73, 93 (left center), 94, 99 (right), 103 (top right), 104 (right), 106 (bottom), 107 (left center), 115 (top left & bottom), 119 (bottom left), 120 (top left & bottom left), 122 (top & bottom right), 138 (bottom), 139 (top left & bottom right), 141; *St. Louis Post-Dispatch:* 68 (left), 79 (left), 102 (top left), 114 (left), 123 (top left), 138 (top left); **Steven Goldstein Photography:** 118 (top right); **Transcendental Graphics:** Mark Rucker Collection, 12 (bottom right), 35 (left center), 41 (left)

Photography: Dan Donovan Photography; PDR Productions, Inc.

Colorizing: Wilkinson Studio, Inc.

The St. Louis Cardinals, winners of the 1982 World Series, proudly display their world-championship trophy.

Contents

Rogers Hornsby

Knothole Gang Pass

Stan Musial

Bob Gibson

Lou Brock Ball

Albert Pujols

FOREWORD

Wearing the St. Louis Cardinals' uniform was an honor for me. I thanked God every day for the opportunity to play major-league baseball and for letting me be lucky enough to spend 15 seasons as a Cardinal.

Very few franchises in baseball can match the Cardinals' tradition. Some of the greatest players in the history of the game have worn the Birds on the Bat. They include Stan Musial, Bob Gibson, Lou Brock, and many others.

The team's tradition was one of the first things I thought about when I was traded from San Diego to St. Louis before the 1982 season. I knew I was coming to a franchise that had won multiple World Series, where the fans were considered the "best in baseball," and where I would have an opportunity to become the best baseball player I could be.

I was not born with great size or strength, and I knew at an early age that if I was going to make my dream of playing in the major leagues a reality, the only way to do it would be through hard work and dedication—willing myself to become the best player I could be.

Growing up, I tried to develop my defensive skills. When a friend was available, we played catch. When I was alone, I created games to challenge myself. I bounced balls off the concrete steps in front of our house; moving closer all the time, I had to react faster and faster if I wanted to catch the ball. I also tested myself by throwing a ball high in the air, over our house, then running from the frontyard to the backyard to try to get there in time to catch the ball. I never did, but I never stopped trying.

I think that was the secret to my success—I never stopped trying, even after I made it to the major leagues. I always wanted to be the best player I could be and be known for more than my defensive skills.

In my first season with the Cardinals, my manager, Whitey Herzog, came up with an idea to help me become a better hitter—he promised to pay me a dollar every time I hit the ball on the ground, even if it resulted in an out. If I hit the ball in the air, I owed him a dollar. Whitey knew that with my speed I would reach base far more often on ground balls than fly balls. I accepted the challenge, and I think I was about $300 ahead when Whitey called off the deal later that year.

It is kind of ironic that even though I won 13 consecutive Gold Gloves from 1980 to 1992, the one singular play of my career that most people remember came as a hitter—in the ninth inning of Game 5 of the 1985 National League Championship Series against the Dodgers.

Facing reliever Tom Niedenfuer, I batted left-handed . . . and hit the first home run of my career from that side of the plate. The homer gave us a 3–2 victory and put us just one win away from the World Series.

More than twenty years later, more than ten years after I retired, and more than five years after I was elected to the Hall of Fame, that highlight is still aired quite often, not just in St. Louis but around the country. One of the reasons, I know, is that it also turned out to be one of the most famous calls in broadcaster Jack Buck's Hall of Fame career. He told the fans to "go crazy folks, go crazy."

My goal that day was not to win the game with a home run. My goal was the same every day I wore a major-league uniform—to be the best player I could be. There was not a single day when I took my status as a major-leaguer for granted.

Hundreds of players have shared my honor of wearing a Cardinals uniform. You will read about many of them in this colorful and exciting book, and you will be able to relive all of the special moments that have added to the legacy and tradition of this wonderful franchise.

I was fortunate to be part of the story.

—Ozzie Smith

CHAPTER ONE

THE EARLY YEARS
1892–1912

THE GREENING OF professional baseball in St. Louis was—from brown to red—a colorful process. As the Browns, the city's franchise realized enormous success in the 1880s. But when the club joined the new National League in 1892, its fortunes fell like a Bob Gibson curveball. The 20th century brought a new name—the Cardinals—but victories remained elusive.

New Sportsman's Park
SCORE BOOK
(OFFICIAL)
Championship Games National League and American Association.

Simmons Hardware Co
210 North Broadway

FURNISH the BROWNS with Uniforms and
Supplies, and ARE HEADQUARTERS for
ALL BASE BALL GOODS,
FIRE ARMS, BICYCLES, FISHING TACKLE,
LAWN TENNIS, and
GENERAL SPORTSMEN'S SUPPLIES.

The Browns use the celebrated Louisville Slugger Bats.

Simmons Hardware Co
210 North Broadway

Above: The "Cardinals" were still known as the Browns in 1895, when the team lost 92 games and employed four different managers.

Right: The 1885 Browns (shown here) won their first of four consecutive American Association pennants.

Right: Mustaches weren't mandatory, but perhaps they helped the 1883 St. Louis Brown Stockings (who later became the Cardinals). The Brown Stockings were 65–33 in the American Association.

BULLETIN. INNINGS
LOUIS. 123456789
INNINGS
METROPOLITAN
ATHLETICS
CINCINNATI.
COLUMBUS

9

Learning to Fly

According to the St. Louis Cardinals media guide, the franchise officially came into existence in 1892. The game of baseball, however, had begun to dig its claws into the city's culture perhaps a half-century earlier (at least on children's playgrounds), and even as the Civil War raged, amateur clubs were forming.

Ironically, it was these squads' ineptitude, not their success, that spawned the embryonic Cardinals. Drubbings—often by margins of 20 to 40 or more runs—at the hands of such early touring professional teams as the Cincinnati Red Stockings and Chicago White Stockings were unbecoming of such a proud, pulsating city. In 1874, a group of well-heeled boosters raised $20,000 to join the National Association, called their team the Brown Stockings, and set about populating their roster with players. Among them were such pioneers as Lipman Pike (a veteran of the mid-'60s Philadelphia A's who some have called the first professional "baseballer") and Edgar

"Ned" Cuthbert (often cited as the "inventor" of the slide).

The Brown Stockings, who wore brown socks—or perhaps white ones soiled by spat tobacco juice, as a quaint legend has it—played their games at the Grand Avenue Grounds, later known as Sportsman's Park. And while success in their inaugural 1875 season was modest, a couple of wins over the despised White Stockings bred a fervor that endures to this day among St. Louis's legendarily zealous fans. Those epic battles created horse-and-buggy traffic jams the likes of which had never been seen. The ballpark spilled over with as many as 10,000 spectators, and the ensuing victories sent the denizens into a frenzy of all-night revelry.

"With all the bragging of that boastful city," wrote a *St. Louis Republican* scribe of the vanquished Chicagoans, "the result only illustrates once more the old truth that bluster

Above: The American Association struck a blow for parity when, in 1886, its champion (the Brown Stockings) defeated the National League champion (the White Stockings, who later became the Cubs).

Below: The 1909 Cardinals (pictured here at Robison Field) were one of the more inept outfits in franchise history. They suffered through a 54–98 season.

Above: Walter "Arlie" Latham was a renowned jokester who once exploded a firecracker under the third base bag to "wake himself up."

does not always win. In this, as other things, St. Louis proves stronger." The gauntlet had been thrown down. Baseball was as much an ingredient of life in the Gateway City as steamboats and beer.

The years that immediately followed were a free-for-all of false starts, player raids, league-jumping, bizarre management, scandal, and—against all odds—competitive success. The National Association folded, upon which the Browns became a member of the original National League. After operating as an independent team for a time, they joined the American Association, winning four straight pennants and two World Series from 1885 to 1888.

A cavalcade of characters passed through St. Louis in those days. There was pot-bellied pitcher/glassblower George "Jumbo" McGinnis, who won 88 games and then flamed out. Tom Parrott coated his skin with iodine before games. Tony Mullane, a 35-game winner in 1883, was a heartthrob and a temperamental pain in the posterior. Third baseman Arlie Latham was a vaudeville performer in the off-seasons and future pickle salesman, who (with apologies to Ozzie Smith) was the first Cardinal to do flips on the field. In 1883, two drunken players attacked manager Ted Sullivan. Outfielder Curt Welch once was hauled off to jail in the middle of a game.

Things were not nearly as sanguine for the Browns after the American Association disbanded in 1891. After being invited into a reformulated National League, they finished no higher than ninth place until 1899, a season in which the reeling club was eye-rollingly renamed the Perfectos.

By the end of the century, Frank and Stanley Robison bought the team and, seeking a fresh start and a refurbished image, ditched the brown socks and replaced them with vivid red. That—and a comment from a fan—inspired sportswriter Willie McHale to christen the club the "Cardinals." The moniker stuck, and a page was turned. A team that struggled to win more than a third of its National League games in the 19th century commenced its agonizingly slow transformation into the most successful franchise in the history of the National League.

American Association star James "Tip" O'Neill is the only player ever to win the Triple Crown (.435-14-123 in 1887) yet not get elected to baseball's Hall of Fame.

A DIFFERENT SET OF RULES

The baseball rule book was a moving target when the Cardinals were fledglings. In 1887, for example, when St. Louis outfielder James "Tip" O'Neill finished with what then was recorded as a .492 batting average, bases on balls were counted as hits. Granted, five balls constituted a walk—but it took four strikes to strike out. Still, it wasn't a bad year for O'Neill, who smacked .435 even after walks were removed from his stats.

Hitters in general had certain advantages in this era. Defenders played with fingerless gloves or no gloves at all. Pitchers were prohibited from throwing overhand until the mid-1880s—though the distance between the mound and plate (which, by the way, was round) was less than the current 60 feet, 6 inches until 1893. From 1887 to 1891, bats were allowed to have one flat side, but this kind of bat was officially outlawed in 1893. At least in the Browns' first professional season of 1875, someone named Fred Thayer had the good sense to invent the catcher's mask.

"Coney Island of the West"

Grand Avenue Grounds in St. Louis was merely an open lot that first saw a white sphere soar across its patchy green in the 1860s. From 1875 to 1877, the Brown Stockings found it suitable enough to inhabit, but when the club dropped out of the original National League, the field was abandoned. It was unimaginable at the time, but the game of baseball would come to be played at the corner of Grand and Dodier longer than on any other site in the world.

When the Browns joined the American Association in 1882, the Sportsman's Park and Club Association renovated and renamed the Grand Avenue Park. William and Al Spink headed the Association, and brother Al became famous as the founder of *The Sporting News*. This new facility was the original Sportsman's Park and was distinguished by its open beer garden in right field, less than 300 feet from the batter's box. It was common for diners to scramble out of their chairs as an outfielder pursued a live ball through the establishment.

Such intimate charm was replaced by a frontal assault of stimulation when owner Chris Von der Ahe moved his charges to Vandeventer and Natural Bridge in 1893. New Sportsman's Park was about much more than just baseball. Dubbed the "Coney Island of the West," there were amusement rides, fireworks, lawn bowling, handball courts, water chutes, Civil War reenactments, Wild West shows, and horse races.

But on April 16, 1898, merriment turned to misery. During a game with the Cubs, fire swept through the park. Most of the 6,000 spectators rushed toward the lone, nonengulfed exit only to find it locked. They then battered down the doors to escape. At least 100 people suffered burns and broken bones, but miraculously no one perished. Several of the players performed heroic acts, but not only did Von der Ahe force them to clear the rubble that evening, they also had to play the next day's game. His intrepid Browns made 11 errors and lost 14–1.

Fans in the grandstands saw the St. Louis Browns play the Chicago White Sox on a rough field at the old Sportsman's Park.

Above: Can anyone here manage this team? Apparently *everyone* could manage in early baseball—even Cardinals owner Stanley Robison, who tried his hand at it for a time in 1905 and went 19–31.

Left: Al Spink, who in 1910 wrote a seminal history of baseball, worked for the 19th-century Brown Stockings until he left to start an eight-page weekly newspaper whose first edition hit the streets on St. Patrick's Day, 1886. He called it *The Sporting News*.

Von der Ahe and the Robisons

Take a heapin' helpin' of George Steinbrenner, a dollop of Marge Schott, and a pinch of Charlie Finley, and you come up with a close approximation of Chris Von der Ahe, the Browns' owner from 1881 to 1899. At his best, he was well liked by most of his players and a pioneer who was a whiz at marketing the game to fans. At worst, he was an insufferable meddler of questionable scruples, ever-flanked in his dandified garb by his pair of pet greyhounds and almost totally void of knowledge of the game.

It was Von der Ahe, however, who betrothed the still-inseparable couple of beer and baseball in St. Louis. A tavern owner who more or less purchased the Browns as a vehicle to sell more grog, he defied the puritanical establishment of the sport by offering it for sale at games. Within a few years, Sportsman's Park was "the place to be" in St. Louis, the Browns were dominating the American Association, and their eccentric owner was the toast of the town.

Eventually, Von der Ahe crumpled under an avalanche of debt, lawsuits, spectacular interpersonal foibles,

Team owner Chris Von der Ahe grudgingly moved the Browns from the American Association to the National League, and initially it turned out to be a financial disaster.

Helene Robison married Schuyler Britton, a Cleveland attorney.

and even his own kidnapping by a private detective impersonating a sportswriter. Enter the Robison brothers, Frank and Stanley, owners of the National League's Cleveland Spiders, a competitive but far less lucrative franchise. The Robisons bought the Browns, changed their name to the Cardinals, then promptly "traded" the Spiders' best players (such as Hall of Famers Cy Young and Jesse Burkett) to St. Louis for inferior ones to capitalize on the stronger market. The ploy turned the 39–111 club of 1898 into an 84–67 upstart in 1899.

In 1911, ownership of the franchise passed through inheritance to 32-year-old Helene Hathaway Robison Britton, daughter of Frank. "Lady Bee," as she was known, horrified the sport's chauvinistic power structure with her proactivity in Cardinals affairs. Although she was cash-strapped and had to sell out in 1917 with the club playing (very badly) to mostly empty seats, Britton established her place in history as the first woman to own a major-league baseball team.

COOLEST NICKNAMES

Long before the phrase "political correctness" became part of the American lexicon, deaf and nearly speechless William Hoy patrolled the St. Louis outfield in 1891. To this day, few know him as anything other than "Dummy." Early baseball nicknames tended to be colorful, brutally descriptive—and abundant. The Cardinals had their share:

Charles "Silver" King (Koenig)
Thomas "Buttermilk Tommy" Dowd
Dave "Scissors" Foutz
William "Bones" Ely
George "Doggie" Miller
William "Klondike" Douglass
R. Emmet "Snags" Heidrick
Clarence "Cupid" Childs
"Tacky" Tom Parrott
Tony "The Apollo of the Box" Mullane
Elton "Icebox" Chamberlain
John "Move Up Joe" Gerhardt
Thomas "Brick" Mansell
Jimmy "Foxy Grandpa" Bannon
Billy "The Little Globetrotter" Earle
George "Piano Legs" Gore
Frank "Dodo" Bird
Charlie "Pretzels" Getzein
Albert "Cowboy" Jones
Charlie "Eagle Eye" Hemphill
John "Trick" McSorley
Pete "Gladiator" Browning
Warren "Hick" Carpenter
"Stooping Jack" Gorman
Mordecai "Three Finger" Brown
Raymond "Chappy" Charles
Herbert "Hub" (or "The Gallatin Squash") Perdue
James "Pud" (or "The Little Steam Engine") Galvin

THE 1928 CARDINALS CLINCHED THE PENNANT ON THE NEXT-TO-LAST DAY OF THE SEASON. "SUNNY" JIM BOTTOMLEY (TOP LEFT) WAS NAMED THE NATIONAL LEAGUE MVP.

CHARLES COMISKEY PLAYED FOR THE BROWNS IN THE 1880S AND 1890S BEFORE LATER GOING ON TO BECOME THE OWNER OF THE CHICAGO WHITE SOX.

ARNOLD HAUSER, WHOSE FACE APPEARS ON THIS BUTTON AND WHOSE NICKNAME "PEE WEE" REFLECTED THE FACT HE STOOD 5'6" AND WEIGHED 145 POUNDS, WAS THE CARDINALS' REGULAR SHORTSTOP FROM 1910 TO 1912.

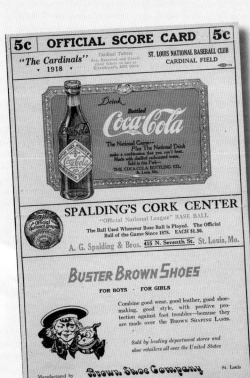

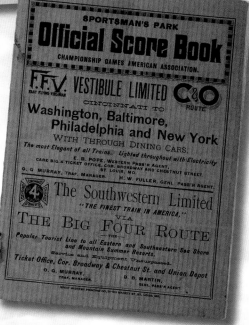

THE CARDINALS FINISHED LAST IN 1918, HAVING LOST 14 PLAYERS TO FIGHT IN WORLD WAR 1. THEY DREW AN ALL-TIME LOW FRANCHISE ATTENDANCE OF 110,000 FANS.

THE 1891 SEASON WAS THE BROWNS' FINAL YEAR IN THE AMERICAN ASSOCIATION, WHICH FOLDED THAT SAME YEAR. FOUR OF THE TEAMS, INCLUDING ST. LOUIS, WERE THEN ADMITTED TO THE NATIONAL LEAGUE IN 1892.

BRANCH RICKEY, WHOSE UNIFORM IS DISPLAYED HERE, SPENT MORE THAN SIX SEASONS AS THE MANAGER OF THE CARDS, FROM 1919 TO 1925, BEFORE ENJOYING FAR GREATER SUCCESS AS THE TEAM'S GENERAL MANAGER.

Early-day Stars

Mordecai "Three Finger" Brown played one season for the Cardinals. At age 7, he'd lost parts of three fingers on his right hand in a corn shredder and, a few weeks later, permanently disfigured the other two when he fell chasing a hog.

Arguably, the "face" of the 19th-century Brown Stockings was player-manager Charlie Comiskey. Signed as a sore-armed pitcher, he talked his way into a switch in 1882 and, according to legendary manager John McGraw, "taught the first basemen how to play the position." The first to "unchain" himself from the bag and patrol the territory situationally, Commy showed off his range in 1887 when he ran down a team of horses that had escaped into Sportsman's Park. It was much later, of course, when Comiskey would make an indelible mark on the game by playing the supporting role of the miserly owner in the Black Sox scandal.

The team's top "power" hitter of this "small-ball" era was Canadian outfielder James "Tip" O'Neill, whose 47 career home runs easily were the most by a pre-National League Browns player. In a remarkable 1887, he hit for the cycle twice in one week and became the first (and still only) player to lead his league in doubles (52), triples (19), and homers (14) in the same season.

The early Browns also featured a pair of the better two-way players in the game's history. From 1884 to 1887, Bob Caruthers and Dave Foutz combined to go 220–86 as pitchers while batting .303. In 1885, one or the other was the starting moundsman in 99 of the team's 112 games.

When, in an impetuous fit, owner Chris Von der Ahe refused to pay his team after it lost the 1887 World Series, his co-aces demanded to be traded and were sold to Brooklyn. That divestiture made young Silver King the team's rotation-topper. In just three years in St. Louis, he labored through more than 1,400 innings and won 111 games—all before his 22nd birthday.

On the last day of the 1891 season for the team's final game in the American Association, the ball was handed to lefty Ted Breitenstein for his first big-league start. The St. Louis "homeboy" promptly no-hit Louisville. He nearly replicated the feat in his next start, taking a no-no into the seventh the following April to deliver the Browns their first NL victory. In 1894, after pitching 34 innings in an eight-day period and throwing a complete game in the opener of a doubleheader on September 9, Breitenstein refused to enter the second game in relief and was suspended.

A number of other prominent players passed through St. Louis with a how-de-do in this era, either in their last throes of greatness or en route to it elsewhere. In the first five loss-infested years of the 20th century alone, the Cardinals discarded eight future Hall of Famers: pitchers Cy Young,

Cy Young claimed only 45 of his record 511 pitching victories while with the Cardinals, leaving St. Louis in a 1901 player raid by the fledgling American League for a salary of $3,500.

Kid Nichols was a better pitcher than manager. He won 21 games as a pitcher in 1904, but the team came away with only 75 victories with him at its helm.

Mordecai "Three Finger" Brown, and Kid Nichols; outfielder Jesse Burkett; catcher Wilbert Robinson; third baseman John McGraw; shortstop Bobby Wallace; and first baseman Jake Beckley. Young and Brown would go on to win 455 more games with a combined ERA of 2.07 for other teams. No player worth his salt, it seemed, wanted to be a Cardinal. So delighted were McGraw and Robinson to escape the incompetence that, during the train ride out of St. Louis following their final game with the team, they pitched their uniforms out the window into the Mississippi River.

No treatise on primitive Redbirds, however, would be complete without addressing this trio of trivia questions:

Who was baseball's pre-Ruth home run champ? On June 3, 1895, aging Browns first baseman Roger Connor passed Harry Stovey to take over the career lead. His 138 four-baggers upon his retirement two years later were sufficient to retain it until the Babe ran him down in 1921.

Who invented the baseball glove? Most credit Bill Doak, who threw spitballs for 13 seasons in St. Louis and sold his design of the modern mitt to the Rawlings Sporting Goods Company in 1919.

And who was the first player known to use a performance-enhancing drug? That would be Pud Galvin, who pitched in eight games for the 1875 Browns before reserving a nook in Cooperstown as baseball's first 300-game

THE FIRST SKIPPERS

Chris Von der Ahe, the Browns' first owner, changed managers—as many as five times in a season, one after only three contests, and another in the middle of a game—as if they were bartenders at his drinking establishment. In fact, the first one he hired—Ned Cuthbert—*was* his bartender. Things stabilized, though, when Von der Ahe appointed no-nonsense Charlie Comiskey. From 1883 to 1891, "The Old Roman" won more than two thirds of his games (excluding managing in the Players League in 1890).

In 1909, Hall of Fame catcher Roger Bresnahan, a player-manager like most in this period, took the reins. In 1911, he may have saved his players' lives. Prior to a train ride to Boston, Bresnahan complained that their seats near the engine were too noisy and demanded their sleeping car be moved to the rear. The train crashed, killing 14 passengers riding in front.

Despite leading the Cardinals to a rare winning season that year, the popular Bresnahan was fired and replaced by second baseman Miller Huggins. "Hug" would enter the Hall of Fame as manager of the dominant 1920s Yankees teams, but he lacked the personnel to succeed in St. Louis.

winner. It is said that, in the latter part of a career in which he completed 646 games, the Pudster kept the ol' wing a-whistlin' by injecting himself with monkey testosterone.

The rosters of the early Cardinal teams were, if not a who's who of the game, at least an entertaining whodunnit. But in 1915, a teenage shortstop named Rogers Hornsby showed up, destined to be the franchise's first megastar.

Miller Huggins (above) was the Cardinals' regular second baseman from 1910 to 1915. He also managed the team from 1913 to 1917 before moving on to the New York Yankees.

Growing Pains and Blunders

Browns owner Chris Von der Ahe, cozy in his American Association comfort zone, wanted no part of the National League when it was reestablished in 1892. But when he refused to match a salary offer of $7,500 to lynchpin Charlie Comiskey by the NL's Cincinnati Reds, his player-manager jumped and took several key players with him. Von der Ahe was corralled into the leagues' merger, but life without Comiskey exposed his limitations as a baseball man, and it would be a long, long time before St. Louis again cheered a winner.

So inept was Von der Ahe at all things baseball that, when he sold the club prior to the 1899 season, the Browns' NL record stood at 316–640. Once, scout Bill Gleason urged him to sign a young third baseman. "Dot liddle feller?" chirped the German immigrant in response. "Take him over to der Fairgrounds and make a horse yockey oudt of him." So John McGraw signed with Baltimore instead.

Still, a grand parade through town hailed the advent of NL ball in St. Louis on April 12, 1892. With Von der Ahe himself calling the shots on the field, the Browns hosted the Chicago Colts (predecessors of the Cubs) and, as would become their custom, got thumped. Five days later, as one of the few teams allowed by local statute to do so, the Browns played the first Sunday game in NL history—a loss to the Reds.

The litany of the team's travails over the next quarter-century is excruciating:

- In 1895, catcher George Miller is so humiliated after throwing away four balls in one *inning* that he resigns as team captain.

- The Browns lose successive 1894 games to the Dodgers by scores of 20–4 and 20–11, with Arthur "Dad" Clarkson surrendering all 20 runs in the first rout. One month later, he allows 21 more to the Phillies.

- In 1896, a fan dies when a boat falls on him at the water slide beyond Sportsman's Park's left-field fence.

- The 1897 season "features" an 18-game losing streak (still the longest in franchise history) as part of a 29–102 debacle.

- In 1899, NL owners extricate the franchise from the debt-ridden Von der Ahe and put it up for auction on the steps of the St. Louis courthouse, where it sells for $33,000.

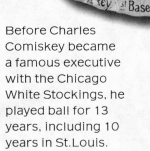

Before Charles Comiskey became a famous executive with the Chicago White Stockings, he played ball for 13 years, including 10 years in St. Louis.

"Cozy" Dolan was a Cardinals outfielder in 1914 and 1915. Acquired in an eight-player deal with the Pirates before the 1914 season, Dolan played for six teams in seven major-league seasons.

- In 1900, Mike Donlin misses two months after a man, who reacts badly to Donlin's barbs about his red beard, stabs him.

- Hundreds of fans at Sportsman's Park storm the field to protest a call by umpire Hank O'Day on July 8, 1901. The police draw revolvers to protect him. Still, he suffers cuts and bruises.

- Before finally defeating him on May 24, 1909, the Cardinals drop 24 consecutive decisions to legendary Giants pitcher Christy Mathewson over a five-year period.

Despite the Cardinals' inauspicious National League nativity, a single sentence in a local newspaper on September 11, 1915, recapping the previous day's game, portended hope. It read: "A 19-year-old Texas kid, Rogers Hornsby, dug up by Bob Connery in the Class-D Western Association, finished the game for the Cardinals at shortstop." It was an innocuous debut: three innings and two hitless at-bats. But on the 14th, the "kid" ripped a single against future Hall of Famer Rube Marquard. It was one hit down, 2,929 more to go.

Hornsby swatted .313 as a full-time player the next season. The year after that marked the arrival of Branch Rickey as team president, and with him, a rare winning record. In 1918, the name "Cardinals" first appeared on the team uniform. In 1919, Rickey assumed the manager's role. The 1920s, as for the rest of America, promised to be roaring in St. Louis.

THE KNOTHOLE GANG

The use of wood to build early ballparks may have presented an unrelenting fire hazard—several conflagrations are part of Sportsman's Park's memoirs—but it was a boon to local kids. Many, unable to pay their way into the game, would spy through holes in the fences to catch a glimpse of their heroes.

In 1917, to link the St. Louis community both financially and emotionally to the Cardinals, anyone who purchased a $25 share of stock in the club could grant a season pass to an underprivileged youngster. The Knothole Gang was born. Not only did the team raise money, but it also hit a public relations grand slam by theoretically addressing the city's juvenile delinquency problem. A new generation of Cardinals fans was being raised.

The Cardinals established the Knothole Gang in 1917, when a section of the stands was reserved for youths who were given a season pass.

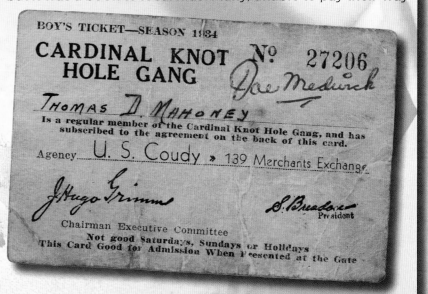

CHAPTER TWO

BUILDING A WINNER
1920–1940

THIRTY-SEVEN YEARS PASSED without a championship in St. Louis. There was little hope that the franchise would be anything more than a money-strapped also-ran in the National League. Then, suddenly, came Rajah and Sunny Jim ... The Fordham Flash and The Wild Horse ... Ol' Pete and Ol' Stubblebeard ... Dizzy, Daffy, and Ducky ... and the man who changed everything for the Cardinals, Branch Rickey.

Sportsman's Park was the home of the Cardinals from 1920 until 1966. When Anheuser Busch bought the Cardinals in 1953, the name of the stadium was changed to Busch Stadium.

In St. Louis, Cubs catcher Leo Hartnett signals the infield before the start of the game on opening day in 1930.

Rogers "Rajah" Hornsby was one of the first true Cardinals stars. He led the Redbirds to their first World Series title in 1926.

The Innovator

The proud tradition of the St. Louis Cardinals was literally pulled out of a hat. After the 1916 season, Barrister Jones, who headed the team's new ownership group, asked seven confidants to write the name of the person they'd recommend for the position of club president on a slip of paper and drop it into his *chapeau*. On every scrap was inked "Branch Rickey." And so the course of the Cardinals, and indeed all of baseball, was radically altered.

A former big-league catcher and then the manager of the AL's St. Louis Browns, Rickey was that rare admixture of intellect and vision. He held four advanced degrees and even passed the West Point entrance exam. Branch could spot the difference between a Hall of Famer and a bush-leaguer before the guy even shaved, and while other executives saw baseball through a telescope, Rickey beheld the game in kaleidoscopic dimensions.

The former Ohio farmboy is generally regarded as the first to assemble a scouting network, to devise an organization-wide teaching system, to compile and utilize statistical probabilities, to employ instructional gadgets, and to organize tryout camps. But his greatest innovation was his notion of the farm system—a concept that transformed the Cardinals from habitual doormats into dynastic champions.

Conceding that they could not compete with the larger-market franchises to purchase players from the independent minor-league clubs, Rickey's master plan was for the Cards to identify, develop, and control their own talent. To that end, he gradually came to own, operate, or otherwise exert influence over a parochial network of farm clubs, stocked with players he and his bird dogs unearthed in almost every cranny of America.

By 1940, Rickey had situated 40 minor-league teams comprised of almost 600 players. Among the "graduates" of his network were great stars such as Jim Bottomley, Chick Hafey, Taylor Douthit, Bill Hallahan, Pepper Martin, Dizzy and Paul Dean, Rip Collins, Joe Medwick, Enos Slaughter, Johnny Mize, Mort and Walker Cooper, Marty Marion, and many more. In fact, every player on the roster of the 1942 world-championship club was signed and developed internally.

Rickey also was the field manager of a series of mediocre

The Cardinals won their first World Series title in 1926, thanks in large measure to the home-grown players who had been signed and developed in the farm system created by Branch Rickey. He earned this ring as the team's general manager.

Branch Rickey, the Cardinals' general manager from 1925-1942, was dubbed—with some irony—"The Mahatma," which is Sanskrit for "Great Soul." Though more opportunistic and smart than "soulful," he was truly a genuine baseball visionary.

Cardinals teams from 1919 to 1925, but that wasn't his forte. Pretty much everything else about running a ballclub was, although he was far from universally popular. Most of his players despised him for his miserly stance in contract negotiations. (Slaughter once said his wealthy boss "would go to the vault to get change for a nickel.") Peers often regarded Rickey as a holier-than-thou hypocrite who was equal parts prudish Bible-thumper, sweet-talking manipulator, and back-stabbing liar as suited his need.

The 1942 season was Rickey's last in St. Louis. Three years later, he would forge his greatest legacy and revolutionize the game yet again by signing Jackie Robinson to play for the Brooklyn Dodgers.

Left: As a player, Rickey did not stand out. In parts of three seasons for the St. Louis Browns, he was a weak hitter and a worse catcher.

RICKEY'S BRILLIANT TRADES

Before Rickey's garden of homegrown talent fully flowered, he kept the Cardinals solvent and competitive by peddling soon-to-decline veterans for cash or diamonds in the rough. Though he had the foresight to turn down big bucks for a young Rogers Hornsby at a time when his club could not afford new uniforms, Rickey was a cunning talent broker.

In 1919, he ratified the last straight player purchase the Cardinals would make until World War II. They had to borrow money to do it, but "B. R." felt the kid righty who'd pitched but one game for Cincinnati was a "can't miss." Jesse Haines would win 210 times for St. Louis in his Hall of Fame career.

In 1926, Rickey virtually certified a championship with two deals in nine June days. First came outfielder Billy Southworth, who would be a terror the rest of the year and later win two more World Series as the Cardinals' manager. Then Rickey arranged a waiver acquisition of pitcher Pete Alexander, hero of the fall classic. That December he finally dealt away a soon-to-decline Hornsby and got back Frankie Frisch, behind whom St. Louis won four pennants.

"Rajah" Hornsby

Only Ty Cobb (.366) owns a higher career batting average than Rogers Hornsby (.358), a player generally regarded as the best right-handed hitter of all time. The Cardinals didn't do a lot of winning during his playing tenure, but he legitimized the franchise.

Cardinals scout Bob Connery considered Rogers Hornsby no more than "a lad who had a chance" when he signed the teen in 1915. Pitchers, as it turned out, had *no* chance. One, Giants lefty Art Nehf, even found the name "A. G. Spalding" tattooed on his chest, courtesy of a line drive off Rajah's incomparable bat.

Hornsby played the first 12 of his 23 seasons in St. Louis. From 1920 to 1925, he hit .397 and won every batting crown. In 1922, he set a league record with 42 home runs and a team mark with a 33-game hitting streak, then swatted .426 two years later. As a player-manager in 1926, he led the franchise to its first World Series title.

Just as importantly, he gave the Cardinals an identity. "He is," wrote reporter J. Roy Stockton in 1926, "the squarest, bluntest, cussingest, and most convincing man I ever met in baseball. He is stubborn, bull-headed, he uses very bad language … but you can't help liking Hornsby."

That wasn't entirely true. Inside the lines, the second baseman was the ultimate competitor. He was so committed that he neither watched movies nor read because he felt it was bad for the eyesight, and he was so obsessive that he skipped his mother's funeral during a pennant race. Off the diamond, he was a disagreeable bigot, a pathetic gambling addict, and an anti-authority irritant who once brawled with Branch Rickey.

Among St. Louis fans, however, Hornsby was passionately popular. They came in record numbers to see him play, and when he was traded after the 1926 season, the mayor of St. Louis filed an official protest. An era had ended for the Cardinals, but a dynasty had begun.

Rogers Hornsby had been a star with the Cardinals in the 1920s. After playing for the Giants, Braves, and Cubs, he returned to the team as a player-coach in 1933 before he was on the move again, this time to the cross-town Browns.

Bunking with the Browns

Reminiscing about his 27 years as owner of the Cardinals, Sam Breadon cited two decisions that reshaped the franchise from doormat to dynasty. One was installing Rogers Hornsby as player-manager in 1925. The second was moving the club back to the original Sportsman's Park. The latter choice had far more enduring implications.

For more than a quarter-century, the facility at Vandeventer and Natural Bridge, which had gone by four names, marked time for the Cardinals. Though it had been renovated on several occasions, Cardinal Field—as it was called from 1917 on—had outlived its usefulness.

In 1920, Breadon had barely taken the reins when he sold it. He conferred part of the proceeds to Branch Rickey to invest in the Cardinals' first farm club, thus triggering the player development system that would transform the team into a powerhouse. Lacking the cash for a new facility, Breadon

In 1926, when the Cards won their first World Series as a member of the National League, Sportsman's Park was "the place to be" in St. Louis. Attendance was 668,248—a franchise record at the time.

TORNADO STRIKES THE BALLPARK

On September 29, 1927, the second-costliest tornado in U.S. history slashed through the St. Louis metropolitan area, killing more than 80 people. Fortunately, the Cardinals were in Cincinnati at the time (where they lost a game that eliminated them from a tight pennant race). Sportsman's Park, however, was not spared.

The twister toppled the pavilion and generally made a mess of the place. The Cards somehow played their final home game two days later, but had the club won the pennant, it was unlikely the World Series could have been staged there.

approached his AL neighbors, the St. Louis Browns—then occupying a spiffed-up Sportsman's Park at Grand & Dodier—about a tenancy. Browns owner Phil Ball wasn't keen at first, but when Breadon (apparently bluffing) announced his intention to construct a *new* park, a deal was struck.

On July 1, 1920, in front of an overflow crowd numbering about 20,000, the Cardinals made their "second debut" there, losing in extra innings to the Pirates. For the next 47 seasons, Sportsman's Park (renamed Busch Stadium in 1953) would house the team with distinction.

Sportsman's Park cost a half-million dollars to refurbish in 1925. Today, that would pay for one third of the Busch Stadium scoreboard.

25

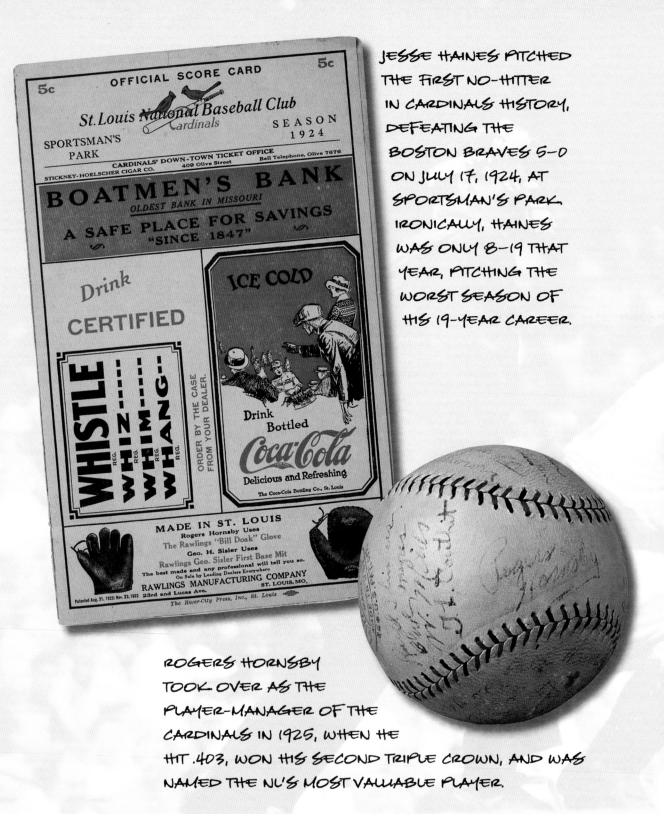

JESSE HAINES PITCHED THE FIRST NO-HITTER IN CARDINALS HISTORY, DEFEATING THE BOSTON BRAVES 5-0 ON JULY 17, 1924, AT SPORTSMAN'S PARK. IRONICALLY, HAINES WAS ONLY 8-19 THAT YEAR, PITCHING THE WORST SEASON OF HIS 19-YEAR CAREER.

ROGERS HORNSBY TOOK OVER AS THE PLAYER-MANAGER OF THE CARDINALS IN 1925, WHEN HE HIT .403, WON HIS SECOND TRIPLE CROWN, AND WAS NAMED THE NL'S MOST VALUABLE PLAYER.

THE FIRST WORLD SERIES GAME EVER PLAYED IN ST. LOUIS WAS ON OCTOBER 5, 1926, THE THIRD GAME OF THE SERIES BETWEEN THE CARDINALS AND YANKEES. THE TWO TEAMS HAD SPLIT THE FIRST TWO GAMES IN NEW YORK. THE CARDINALS WON GAME 3, 4-0, AND WENT ON TO WIN THE SERIES IN SEVEN GAMES.

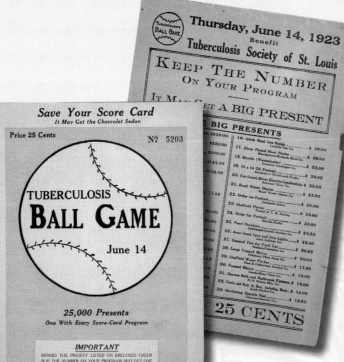

CARDINALS
FIRST BASEMAN
JIM BOTTOMLEY
WAS NAMED THE
LEAGUE'S MVP
IN 1928 AFTER
LEADING THE NL IN
HOME RUNS AND
RBI AND POWERING
THE TEAM TO
ITS SECOND NL
PENNANT IN THREE
YEARS.

JIM BOTTOMLEY
NL most valuable player 1928
"Toasting gives a flavor
no other cigarette
can equal"

TRIPLE CROWN

1922 1925

ROGERS HORNSBY WON THE
TRIPLE CROWN IN BOTH 1922
AND 1925, LEADING THE NL IN
AVERAGE, HOME RUNS, AND
RBI. THE ONLY OTHER PLAYER
IN BASEBALL HISTORY TO
WIN THE TRIPLE CROWN TWICE
IN HIS CAREER WAS TED
WILLIAMS OF THE BOSTON
RED SOX.

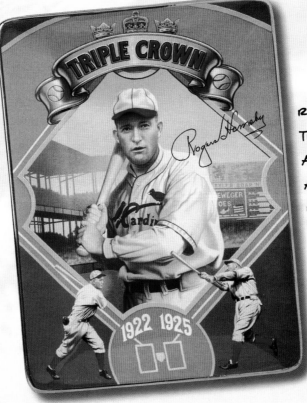

EVEN THOUGH THE CARDINALS
FINISHED FIFTH IN 1923, CARDINAL
FANS STILL SAW ROGERS HORNSBY
WIN ANOTHER NL BATTING TITLE AND
JESSE HAINES PRODUCE A 20-
VICTORY SEASON.

Sunny Jim

It didn't take long for Branch Rickey's tryout camps to pay dividends. One of his first, in 1919, spat out a future Hall of Famer.

Jim Bottomley, a 19-year-old blacksmith's apprentice, showed up wearing his father's street shoes with spikes nailed through the soles. That didn't bother Rickey in the least. "Bottomley, properly shod," said the Cardinals talent guru, "had the grace and reflexes of a great performer."

"Sunny Jim"—so dubbed for his eternally cheerful disposition—was the regular first baseman by 1923, when he hit .371. He followed that with six straight years in which he reached twin digits in doubles, triples, and home runs while knocking in more than 100 teammates. In 1928, he won the MVP Award after leading the league in homers (31), triples (20), and RBI (136). Throughout his career he was a dazzling gloveman, noted especially for recording the final out of the second game of the 1931 World Series by diving over the A's bullpen bench to stab a pop-up.

If the Cardinals have since had a first baseman as good as Bottomley, they never had one more popular. The Knothole Gang kids adored him. More than 10,000 of them showed up for his MVP ceremony. Near the end of his career, he was feted with a special day. Asked what he'd like as a gift, he suggested a cow. That's just what Jim Bottomley got. Its name was Fielder's Choice.

Bottomley's Big Day

Bottomley had a "career" day on September 16, 1924. When the bloodletting ended in the Cardinals' 17–3 romp over the Dodgers, he had filled the RBI column of the box score with a "12." The record total was generated by six hits off five different pitchers. Included were a pair of home runs, one of them a grand slam. It would be 69 years until someone else knocked in a dozen: Mark Whiten—of the St. Louis Cardinals.

From 1924 to 1929, Bottomley drove in more than 100 runs every season—a team record until Albert Pujols went one better in 2007.

Even a lawsuit filed by an inattentive fan who had been struck by one of his home run balls could not dim the perpetual smile of "Sunny Jim" Bottomley.

The First World Title

No one expected much from Rogers Hornsby's nine in 1926. This was the franchise's 35th National League season, and the Cards had never finished higher than third place. The manager had other ideas.

"If there's anybody here who doesn't believe we are going to win, there's a train leaving for the north tonight," Hornsby admonished his players in spring training. But by June, the Cardinals were so mediocre that they had scored 241 runs and allowed 241 runs. The front office swung into action.

Right fielder Billy Southworth arrived and had the year of his life. He solidified a lineup that included 120-RBI man Jim Bottomley and catcher Bob O'Farrell, the NL MVP. The staff was bolstered with the great Pete (Grover Cleveland) Alexander, whom the Cubs had cut loose because they considered him a 39-year-old, washed-up drunk. His first start in St. Louis was phenomenal. He treated the record crowd of 37,196 to a win, and the season seemed to turn. Though forced to close out the campaign with a punishing 25-game road trip, the Cardinals edged the Reds for the "right" to face the mighty Yankees in the World Series.

The combatants split a pair in New York, and upon the return to St. Louis, the *Globe-Democrat* newspaper summed up the scenario suitably, if not succinctly, with this headline: "Greatest Demonstration in City's Baseball History Staged as Frenzied Multitudes Lionize Baseball Heroes Amid Bedlam of Noise and Joyous Enthusiasm."

Despite Babe Ruth disassembling the World Series record book, the Cardinals forced a Game 7. St. Louis nursed a 3–2 lead into the seventh inning, but pitcher Jesse Haines loaded the bases. Alexander had a lot of problems, but pitching was not one of them. Beset by epilepsy and alcoholism, the 350-game winner was known to pass out on the mound. So it was not without trepidation that Hornsby called upon "Ol' Pete"— hungover as usual—for the seven biggest outs in franchise history to that point. He permitted only one runner the rest of the way—that being Ruth, who inexplicably attempted to steal and was thrown out to end the Series and hand the Cardinals a world championship. Two months later, however, euphoria turned to incredulity: Rogers Hornsby was traded.

The 1926 World Series was the only event St. Louis residents were talking about when the Yankees came to town to play the Cardinals.

The St. Louis Chamber of Commerce estimated that more than a million celebrants participated in the feting of the 1926 Cardinals, who conquered the "invincible" New York Yankees in a taut seven-game World Series.

The Fordham Flash

Frankie Frisch was Branch Rickey's kind of player: passionate, horsehide-tough, and the kind of leader his roster of rowdies would defer to. So although Rickey lobbied owner Sam Breadon not to trade Rogers Hornsby after the 1926 season, he was satisfied with the return.

In four consecutive seasons, Frisch had helped the New York Giants reach the World Series, winning twice. His streak of .300 batting averages, at six at the time of the trade, would stretch to 11 in St. Louis. When "The Fordham Flash" hit .337, stole 48 bases, and set a still-standing second base record of 641 assists in his St. Louis debut, Breadon called it the best year he'd ever seen a player have.

Frisch, the 1931 NL MVP for the world-champion Cardinals, retired with

2,880 hits—a record for switch-hitters until Pete Rose came along. And he still holds the modern NL mark of 12 seasons with 500 or more plate appearances and fewer than 20 strikeouts.

For five campaigns, Frisch was the team's respected player-manager, including 1934, when the famed Gashouse Gang tested his patience but won it all. A hobbled Frisch scored his final run three years later and, knowing his career was over, admitted, "I was winded rounding third…my heart pounded… my knees creaked…I touched home plate [and] waved to [the] utility infielder. 'You're a regular now,' I groaned." But no one has ever truly replaced Frisch in St. Louis.

Frankie Frisch overcame the stigma of being "the guy we got for Hornsby" to forge a Hall of Fame career and help the Cards win two world titles. He wasn't the looniest of the bunch, but his hard-nosed approach was definitely the fuel for the Gashouse Gang.

HORNSBY FOR FRISCH

Giants manager John McGraw had been trying to pry Rogers Hornsby from the Cardinals for seven years. His club had offered $300,000 for him when the infielder was just 23. Rickey set his price at a half-million and offered to give New York 50 grand for a rookie he kind of liked—Frankie Frisch. Neither kid changed hands during those negotiations, but by 1926 the Cardinals landscape had changed. Although Rajah had delivered a title, owner Sam Breadon was put off by his star's crude insubordination. When the two reached an impasse on a new contract, Hornsby was dealt to the Giants for Frisch and pitcher Jimmy Ring. Despite the outrage in St. Louis, Frisch quickly placated fans with his Hall of Fame play and became the linchpin on four pennant-winners.

A Cards-Yankees Fall Classic

At its nucleus in the spring, the 1928 team looked a lot like the 1926 champs. But it had one crucial addition.

Rabbit Maranville was a 36-year-old future Hall of Fame shortstop whom Branch Rickey signed a year earlier but sent to the minors to pull himself together. A dazzling defender to pair with Frankie Frisch, Maranville returned in 1928 a new man. "The national consumption of alcoholic beverages took a sharp downturn after May 24, 1927," he declared. "That's the day I quit drinking."

Still, under first-year manager Bill McKechnie, the team was stalled near .500 in May. So Rickey pressed some buttons. A flurry of trades yielded outfielder George Harper, catcher Jimmie Wilson, and the game's only left-handed spitballer, Clarence Mitchell. A 14th-inning homer by Jim Bottomley on June 15 edged the team into first place, where they would remain for all but five days for the rest of the season. September was not without its drama, however, when the team finally eliminated the Giants in its penultimate game.

The 1928 attendance was 778,147, which was a team record for 18 years, and fans hailed a procession of heroes. Jim Bottomley was the Cardinals' third NL MVP in four years, while Frisch was an automaton of excellence. Chick Hafey homered 27 times;

Jesse Haines and Bill Sherdel were 20-game winners; and even Pete Alexander mustered a 16-victory last hurrah.

Regrettably, it was the Yankees, winners of six of the last eight AL flags and bent on revenge for 1926, who would be the World Series opponent. It was no contest. Behind a Babe Ruth-Lou Gehrig tandem that whacked .593 with seven homers, New York swept. An embarrassed Sam Breadon promptly "traded" managers, sending McKechnie to his Triple-A club and calling up Billy Southworth. Eighty-eight games into 1929, he swapped them back, but St. Louis hadn't seen the last of "Billy the Kid."

The Cardinals' 1928 trip to the World Series, their second in three years, once again brought them face-to-face with the Yankees, and this time the result was far less enjoyable. The Yankees won the Series, sweeping all four games.

Named for a president and later portrayed in a movie by a future one (Ronald Reagan), talented and troubled Grover Cleveland Alexander was nearly 40 when he joined the Cardinals. He still went 55–34 in his four-year term with the club.

Cards Storm to World Series

The Cardinals did finally play somebody other than the Yankees in the World Series. In 1930, the Philadelphia A's won the AL pennant and faced the Cardinals, going on to win the Series in six games.

Pundits gave the Cardinals, fresh off a 1929 78–74 yawner, little chance in 1930. But Branch Rickey was confident the core of his fine 1926–1928 units had a pennant or two left in it, and he left it largely undisturbed. For a while.

As in 1928, it was Rickey to the rescue with his procurement of an "over-the-hill" pitcher. With his team's record at 26–28, he traded for 36-year-old Burleigh Grimes, the last pitcher in baseball annals to throw a legal spitball. Like Pete Alexander, Grimes was on the downside of a Hall of Fame career. Unlike "Ol' Pete," "Ol' Stubblebeard" was a fiery—and sober—personality who could elevate a team. And that he did, winning 13 of the 22 games in which he pitched and cultivating a never-say-die attitude.

The Cardinals remained apparently out of the race until mid-August, when they caught fire. By the time they clinched the NL pennant on September 26, they had won 38 of their last 47 games. "You'll go down in baseball history as one of the miracle men of the game," exhorted Frankie Frisch to manager Gabby Street during the locker room celebration.

Come October, the Cards were fresh out of miracles. Neither they nor Connie Mack's defending-champion Philadelphia team batted over .200 in the World Series, but the A's were a clutch bunch in ending St. Louis's season, four games to two.

Despite the setback, the Cardinals were an optimistic lot heading into 1931. A team that had come from farther back than anyone—ever—to win a pennant had an entire lineup of .300 hitters still under contract. For good measure, two brash but promising rookies had sipped a cup of coffee as the curtain fell: a hard-throwing right-hander nicknamed Dizzy and an inelegant but effective outfielder dubbed Pepper.

Al Simmons of the Philadelphia Athletics beats the throw in Game 4 of the 1930 World Series. The Redbirds lose the Series 4–2.

A Dash of Pepper

Before Pete Rose became "Charlie Hustle," Johnny Leonard Roosevelt Martin was "The Wild Horse of the Osage." Martin possessed fewer athletic gifts than many of his contemporaries, but none played with more uninhibited passion. Like Rose, he's not in the Hall of Fame, but many argue he should be.

Branch Rickey happened upon the penniless Oklahoman playing in a Class-D league and assigned him to a club in Arkansas, where the owner anointed him "Pepper." Caught stowed away in a railroad car in an attempt to reach Florida for his first spring training, he spent the night in jail and showed up to camp filthy and disheveled. He would more or less stay that way throughout his career.

Martin was just a rookie in 1931 when he tortured the Athletics with 12 hits, 5 RBI, and an equal number of stolen bases in the World Series. Lucky he didn't get two more hits (which

Pepper Martin has been cited as the "inventor" of the head-first slide—one reason famed sportswriter Red Smith said of him that "no more fiery competitor ever lived in any sport."

A PINCH OF PEPPER

"It was just a *small* bone."
—Martin explaining why he played most of the 1932 season with a broken finger without telling anyone

"[Martin] was so fast, when he went rabbit hunting, he'd outrun the rabbit, overtake it, reach down, and feel how plump it was before deciding whether to put it in his sack or not."
—Branch Rickey

"Pepper was a mess you know. He didn't wear underwear or a jock strap."
—*St. Louis Post-Dispatch* sports editor Bob Broeg to Peter Golenbock in *The Spirit of St. Louis*

"When I want to feel happy I think of him."
—Frankie Frisch on Martin

would have been a Series record), he said later, "because my sombrero mightn't a fit me."

During his 13 years with the Cards, Pepper hit .298, made four All-Star teams, and led the league in stolen bases three times. He also became the ringleader of the madcap Gashouse Gang of 1934, raced midget autos incessantly, went on a vaudeville tour, fired guns from windows, collected hairpins for good luck, and engaged in all other manner of madness. After he left baseball, he became a successful cattle rancher *and* the director of the Oklahoma State Penitentiary—a quirky contradiction to the end.

Pepper's stats were nothing to sneeze at (his .418 World Series batting average is fourth all time), but it was his salty personality that defined the screwy image of the 1934 world-champion Gashouse Gang.

Cards Win a Thrill-packed Classic

Frankie Frisch described the Birds of 1931 as "happily efficient." Both he and manager Gabby Street deemed them the best team they'd ever been associated with. The NL's sole 100-game winner in a 21-year period had its share of stand-by stars: NL MVP Frisch, Jim Bottomley, batting champ Chick Hafey, Bill Hallahan (the NL wins and strikeouts leader), and Burleigh Grimes.

But if the Cards' pennant cruise was white noise, the World Series rematch against Philadelphia was a fire alarm. Its only ho-hum moment was an easy A's win in the opener. Otherwise Pepper Martin would make sure that the Cards were on fire.

He manufactured the only runs of Game 2 with a pair of hits, stealing a base and scoring both times to support Hallahan's shutout. When the Series switched to Philadelphia, the "Wild Horse" singled, doubled, and scored twice, while Grimes spun a two-hitter. Pepper popped the team's

only pair of hits in a Game 4 defeat, then he homered, singled twice, and drove in four runs as the Redbirds took a three-games-to-two edge in Game 5.

After the A's evened the series, it was back to a quaking Sportsman's Park for the deciding game. Behind a jumble of lucky hits, A's misplays, a sacrifice, a walk, a wild pitch, a steal, and the most important home run of George Watkins's career, St. Louis jumped to a 4–0 lead by the third inning. Grimes came within one out of a shutout but allowed two runs before Hallahan induced the potential tying run to line out to—who else?—Pepper Martin to end the game. The Cards became world champs for a second time.

Burleigh Grimes twice lost shutouts in the ninth inning of 1931 World Series games—one on a home run by Philly's Al Simmons (here greeted by team-mates)—but won both games anyway.

GABBY STREET

Whether regaling his players with tales of his World War I service or bantering with Harry Caray in the Cardinals radio booth of the 1940s, Charles Street was "Gabby." The charmingly loquacious Alabaman once pocketed $500 by catching a baseball dropped from the top of the Washington Monument on his 15th try. He was requiem-serious about baseball, though—being the only manager in the franchise's first half-century to win back-to-back pennants. By mid-1933, ill-suited to abide the shenanigans of the soon-to-be Gashouse Gang, he was—to his own relief—replaced by Frankie Frisch.

The Gashouse Gang

St. Louis Post-Dispatch reporter J. Roy Stockton authored this 1945 account of the Cardinals' wackos, which included Leo Durocher (left) and Frankie Frisch (right).

The story goes that sportswriter Frank Graham overheard a conversation between Leo Durocher and Dizzy Dean in 1933. Diz speculated that the sixth-place Cardinals could win the pennant if they were in the American League. "They wouldn't let us *in* the other league," replied the scruffy, tobacco-spitting Durocher, glancing at a spit-shined Yankees team going through warm-ups. "They would say we are a lot of gas house ballplayers." The term "Gashouse Gang" had bored its way into the baseball lexicon.

The kooky coterie of Cardinals cultivated its image as a horde of hard-living, practical-joking, childlike, cheeky dirtbags. There was loopy Pepper Martin, the unpredictable Dizzy Dean, the acerbic Durocher, playboy and surreptitious ring-leader Ripper Collins, and Ernie "Showboat" Orsatti, a former Hollywood stuntman. With this band of merry mischief-makers, player-manager Frankie Frisch had his hands full, but his own voracious, win-or-else demeanor qualified even him as a certified Gang member.

From trashing hotels to brawling with opponents to snipering with water balloons, the Gashouse Gang was more than a team; it was a culture. The players refused to wash their uniforms during a winning streak. Martin would cloud the clubhouse with sneezing powder, singe a teammate with a hotfoot, infest a hairdo with chewing gum, or spit tobacco into an abandoned glove. He and Dean once crashed a high-society luncheon by throwing smoke bombs into a hotel ballroom, then rushing in impersonating firefighters. In Philadelphia, a band of Gashousers tossed a string of firecrackers into the front end of a total stranger's Rolls-Royce and slammed the hood shut.

Then there was the famous Mudcat Band, which belted out hillbilly music while attired in cowboy garb and sombreros. Martin was out front playing guitar and harmonica, and several Cardinals chimed in with fiddles, jugs, and washboards. The combo would even appear in nightclubs, hammering out such tunes as "Willie, My Toes Are Cold" and "They Buried My Sweetie Under an Old Pine Tree."

In his later years, Frisch finally admitted, "They drove me nuts." Then he added, "But if I could have a bunch like that every year, I'd be quite content to stay nuts."

Top left: This could only be the Gashouse Gang, with Pepper Martin in the front of the line as usual.

The catchy nickname for the Cardinals' teams in the 1930s is credited to Frank Graham, a sportswriter with the *New York Sun*. Here is a page from one of his features.

Daffy and Dizzy

For the 1934 champion Cards, Daffy (left) and Dizzy Dean set a record for most victories (49) by sibling teammates. They then accounted for every Cardinals win in the World Series.

In 1930, a 20-year-old prospect called Dizzy was warming up prior to his big-league debut when the mayor of St. Louis approached manager Gabby Street. "Is he going to be as good as they say?" Victor Miller inquired. "I think he's going to be a great one, Mr. Mayor," replied Street. "But I'm afraid we'll never know from one minute to the next what he's going to do or say."

Gabby got *that* right.

Dean mesmerized the Pirates with a three-hitter that day, then returned in 1932 to start a six-season run during which he was baseball's leading winner and greatest strikeout pitcher. He also ran amuck like a toddler on road trips, whined incessantly about his compensation, made outrageous statements in his fractured English, and mocked opponents ("Son, what kind of pitch would you like to miss?").

Ol' Diz, however, had a serious right arm.

Five straight seasons he rung up at least 18 wins and 190 strikeouts. On July 30, 1933, he blew away 17 Cubs (then a record). No National Leaguer has won 30 games since Dean did it in 1934, when he was MVP.

That season Diz was joined by his younger brother Paul, who was expediently but inappropriately nicknamed "Daffy." The more serene sibling spun two quick 19-win seasons and was a World Series star. In one twin bill, Dizzy dealt a shutout in the opener and Paul fired a no-hitter in the nightcap.

Both Deans, however, were washed up prematurely because of arm injuries. Paul was essentially done at 23. Diz, despite only three wins after he turned 30, made it to Cooperstown where, in his induction speech, he famously thanked the Lord for "a strong body, a good right arm, and a weak mind."

Dizzy Dean's brother Paul, given the nickname Daffy, joined his older brother on the Cardinals' staff in 1934. That same year, Dizzy was named the league's MVP.

Dean Duo Tames the Tigers

By the summer of 1933, Gabby Street had been replaced as manager by Frankie Frisch, and heroes such as Jim Bottomley, Chick Hafey, and Paul Derringer were gone. It was just Dizzy being dizzy, most thought, when he predicted the Birds would win it all in 1934. The Dean boys would win 45 games all by themselves, he promised. For perhaps the only time in his life, Dizzy underestimated himself.

"Your nights are your own, but your days belong to me," Frisch cautioned his rowdy roster. "We haven't any room for softies." The Gashouse Gang was anything but soft. The entire season was a grueling climb to overtake the potent New York Giants. The Gang caught fire in August, but were still six games out on Labor Day.

The Deans took it from there. During the final week they pitched nearly every day.

From September 21 to 30, indefatigable Dizzy won four starts, three by shutout. Helped by a Giants collapse, the last of those clinched the pennant. Dizzy and Paul Dean had combined for 49 of the team's 95 wins.

The World Series against the Tigers mirrored the tension of the regular season. Diz dispatched Detroit in the opener, 8–3, behind Joe Medwick's bat. Game 2 was lost in the 12th, but Paul won back in St. Louis.

After five of his pitchers were shelled in Game 4, Frisch decided it would be all Deans, all the time. The brothers didn't let him down. Although Diz lost a well-pitched Game 5, Paul bailed him out the next day. The rubber match was over in a hurry: The Cardinals scored seven times in the third inning, and Dizzy took it from there in an 11–0 shutout. The Gashouse Gang had secured its legacy.

The motto of Grunow Radio Company was "Radio That Actually Lives!" The hard-scrabble 1934 Cardinals actually lived their reputation as a bunch of ill-mannered, aesthetically challenged, but indomitable underdogs.

THE CARDINALS OVERCAME A THREE-GAMES-TO-TWO DEFICIT TO
COME BACK AND BEAT THE TIGERS AND WIN THE 1934 WORLD
SERIES, WINNING THE FINAL TWO GAMES IN DETROIT.

AFTER LOSING THE
1930 WORLD SERIES TO
THE PHILADELPHIA A'S,
THE TWO TEAMS MET
AGAIN THE FOLLOWING
YEAR. PEPPER MARTIN
HIT .500 WITH 12 HITS IN
THE SERIES, LEADING
THE CARDINALS TO THE
CHAMPIONSHIP IN SEVEN
GAMES.

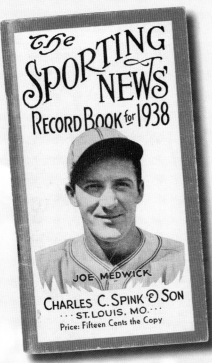

THERE WAS NO MORE POPULAR TEAM IN BASEBALL IN THE 1930S THAN THE CARDINALS, WHO COMBINED THEIR COLORFUL PLAYERS WITH SUCCESS, WINNING THREE NL PENNANTS AND TWO WORLD SERIES TITLES. GEORGE M. COHAN, A GREAT AMERICAN COMPOSER AND ENTERTAINER LIVING IN THE EARLY 20TH CENTURY, PAID TRIBUTE TO THE CARDINALS WITH HIS MUSIC.

JOE MEDWICK WAS THE TOAST OF THE NATIONAL LEAGUE IN 1938 AFTER WINNING THE LEAGUE'S TRIPLE CROWN THE PREVIOUS YEAR. HE SET A FRANCHISE RECORD WITH 154 RBI AND WAS NAMED THE NL MOST VALUABLE PLAYER. MEDWICK REMAINS THE LAST NL PLAYER TO EVER WIN THE TRIPLE CROWN.

THE LORE OF DIZZY DEAN REMAINED LONG AFTER HIS PLAYING CAREER ENDED. EVEN THOUGH HE SPENT ONLY SIX FULL SEASONS IN A CARDINALS UNIFORM, HE REMAINS ONE OF THE LEGENDARY PLAYERS IN FRANCHISE HISTORY.

Ducky Medwick

Joe Medwick was an odd duck. But that's not where he got his nickname. Called "Ducky" because of a waddling stride, he was called worse for his egomania, hostility, avarice, and thin skin.

The Cardinals' star left fielder throughout the 1930s, however, was lionized for his unadulterated ability to hit. His batting average topped .350 three straight years, and he eclipsed 100 RBI six years in a row. From 1933 to 1937 he never racked up fewer than 40 doubles, 10 triples, and 18 homers.

The prickly son of Hungarian immigrants had little use for the Gashouse Gang's monkeyshines. He slugged at least two of his teammates, threatened Dizzy Dean with a bat, and especially loathed the Mudcat Band, once complaining, "What the hell are we anyway, a ballclub or a minstrel show?"

Medwick made ten All-Star teams (six while with St. Louis) and the Hall of Fame. But in 1940, less than a week after he was traded to the Dodgers, he was badly beaned by the Cards' Bob Bowman in apparent retaliation for a feud between the pitcher and Brooklyn manager Leo Durocher. He was never quite the same.

"I have two good friends in the world, the buckarinos and the base hits," Ducky once said. "If I get the base hits, I will get the buckarinos." Medwick mellowed later in life, passing away at 63 with 2,471 hits, enough buckarinos, and more friends than he'd admit to.

Joe Medwick, who preferred the nickname "Muscles" to the more common "Ducky," didn't make the Hall of Fame until two decades after his retirement, perhaps because of his antagonistic relationship with the sports media. "It was like a 20-year slump," he said when he was informed of his election. In 1944, the irreverent, edgy "Ducky" met Pope Pius XII, who asked him what his vocation was. "I'm Joe Medwick," he replied. "I, too, used to be a Cardinal."

TRIO OF TRIPLE CROWNS

The Triple Crown is such a rare achievement that there have been only six in National League history. Three were by Cards. In 1922, Rogers Hornsby pulled off the first of the modern era, leading the NL in batting average (.401), home runs (42), and RBI (152). Three years later he did it again (.403-39-143). Joe Medwick added his name to the short list in 1937 (.374-31-154). Ironically, there was only one in the old American Association. That was done by St. Louis's Tip O'Neill in 1887.

The Big Cat

Some of Branch Rickey's best, worst, and luckiest decisions involved Johnny Mize. The best was to sign him in the first place. The broad-shouldered Georgian first played organized ball as a high schooler for the team of a small college at which he was never enrolled. Years later, Rickey's brother Frank actually plucked the first baseman off a lumber company squad in Georgia.

Branch's worst move was to sell Mize to the Reds before he ever reached the major leagues. The luckiest was to get him back four months later when Cincinnati claimed he was damaged goods because of a hip injury.

"The Big Cat" played six seasons in St. Louis, driving home at least 93 runs in each. He won the 1939 batting crown at .349 and led the league in homers that year and the next, with 28 and 43, respectively. Unlike most sluggers, Mize rarely struck out, topping 50 in a season but once.

"Mize was a great, great hitter," remembers Ralph Kiner, the only man of the era who rivaled Johnny as a slugger. "I think of him and [Stan] Musial alike, great average hitters who used the whole field."

Rickey would make one more ill-advised decision: not to offer Mize near what he was worth in salary. When the future Hall of Famer balked, he was traded to the Giants for three journeymen and cash in 1941. Unfortunately for the Cardinals, he had another 201 home runs in him, playing past his 40th birthday and inspiring this verse from sportswriter Dan Parker: "Your arm is gone, your legs likewise; But not your eyes, Mize, not your eyes."

Above: In Johnny Mize's era, Americans (unaware of health risks) considered it suave to smoke. It was common for baseball stars to endorse tobacco products whether they used them or not.

Right: For a big man with raw-boned power, Johnny Mize moved gracefully and relied as much on studying pitchers as his brute strength. He is the only man to hit three home runs in a game six times.

First baseman Johnny Mize led the National League with 43 homers in 1940, which remained the Cardinals' single-season record until Mark McGwire shattered the mark in 1998.

CHAPTER THREE

STAN "THE MAN" AND CO.
1941–1959

ONE-TIME CARDINALS CATCHER Jimmie Wilson, the Cubs manager in 1941, had just watched a 20-year-old outfielder playing his first week in the bigs dismantle his team in a doubleheader by rapping six hits (including two doubles and a bunt), scoring a winning run from second on an infield squib, throwing out a runner at home, stealing a base, and making two diving catches. "Nobody but *nobody* can be that good," he said. But Wilson could be absolved of his skepticism; at one time even the Cardinals had underestimated Stan Musial.

The 1942 Redbirds, here following the last out of their World Series upset of the Yankees, were a tight-knit, and perhaps overachieving, bunch.

No Cardinal was more popular than Stan Musial during his playing career, and advertisers hoped his connection with the fans would prompt them to buy whatever product Musial was endorsing.

The 1943 World Series was a rematch of the St. Louis Cardinals and the New York Yankees from the previous year. Game 3 was played at Yankee Stadium on October 7, 1943, in which the Bronx Bombers rallied in the bottom of the eighth inning to upend the Redbirds.

Baseball's Perfect Knight

The son of impoverished Eastern European immigrants living in Pennsylvania, Stan Musial was signed in 1938 as a left-handed pitcher for the St. Louis Cardinals. Wildness and a shoulder injury provoked more than one recommendation for his release, but he was given a last-ditch look as a Class-C outfielder in 1941. Within months, he was dazzling manager Billy Southworth in St. Louis with his ability and astonishing instincts for the game.

Installed as the Cards' left fielder in 1942, Musial commenced a run of 16 consecutive seasons—seven of which bore batting titles—in which he never hit below .310. With maturity came more pop, and Stan would retire in 1963 with 475 home runs and 6,134 total bases—a sum exceeded in baseball history only by Hank Aaron. There were a trio of MVP Awards, 24 All-Star Game invitations, three World Series crowns, and, ultimately, a body of work that places him prominently in the discussion as one of the finest players of all time.

Musial is also in the running as the finest gentleman ever to play the game. Unfailingly professional, kind, and humble, he will forever be the "face" of the Cardinals organization, whether the criterion be performance or personality.

"Sometimes the respect for and feeling about Stan reached such proportions that his teammates actually felt that with Stan around nothing bad could happen to them," says Tim McCarver, a teammate late in Musial's career.

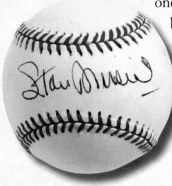

Every avid Cardinals fan either covets or owns an autographed Musial ball. Having him sign the ball in person is a memory they will always cherish.

Musial's "weapon" of choice was the Louisville Slugger M159. The company still produces the model today.

Musial adopted an unusual stance—closed, crouched, and with a little hula-dance wiggle to settle in—because he felt it gave him better plate coverage.

Of the understated superstar, sportscaster Bob Costas has acclaimed, "All Musial represents is more than two decades of sustained excellence and complete decency as a human being."

After retirement, Stan became a successful businessman, and, in a brief stint as Cardinals general manager, traded for Roger Maris, who was instrumental in the team's 1967 world championship. Since 1968, "No. 6" has stood immortalized in bronze outside of Busch Stadium, his statue inscribed with these words from former commissioner Ford Frick: "Here stands baseball's perfect warrior. Here stands baseball's perfect knight."

The club formally recognized Stan Musial as the embodiment of all things Cardinal with the erection of a bronze statue outside Busch Stadium in 1968.

HERE COMES THE MAN

Brooklyn Dodgers pitcher Carl Erskine, asked how he pitched to Musial, responded, "I've had pretty good success by throwing him my best pitch and backing up third." So weary were Dodgers fans of seeing their pitchers back up third when Stan came to town that, out of respect for his greatness, there was an unspoken Ebbets Field canon that he should never be booed. "Uh oh," they would mutter in Brooklyn when Musial approached the plate, "Here comes the man again. Here comes the man." St. Louis scribe Bob Broeg picked up on the mantra, and the descriptive nickname Stan "The Man" stuck. "He'd kill you," remembered Boston Braves hurler Johnny Sain. "But he was a gentleman."

STANLEY FRANK MUSIAL
"THE MAN"
ST. LOUIS CARDINALS 1941-1963
HOLDS MANY NATIONAL LEAGUE RECORDS,
AMONG THEM: GAMES PLAYED 3026; AT
BAT 10972 TIMES; 3630 HITS; MOST RUNS
SCORED 1949; MOST RUNS BATTED IN 1951;
TOTAL BASES 6134. LED N.L.IN TOTAL
BASES 6 YEARS, SLUGGING PERCENTAGE
6 YEARS. MOST VALUABLE PLAYER 1943-
1946-1948. PLAYED IN 24 ALL-STAR GAMES.
LIFETIME BATTING AVERAGE .331.

The 106-win Season

If the 1934 Gashouse Gang was a clamorous cacophony, the 1942 Cardinals were symphonic harmony. They played the game hard and tough, and there were few pranksters and little off-the-field drama. All had come up through Branch Rickey's farm system, everyone got along famously, and they could flat play the game. The team was an exquisite mélange of hitting, pitching, speed, and defense, masterfully manipulated by manager Billy Southworth, who had, two years before, been recalled from his banishment to the minors.

The outfield and the pitching staff were bedrock. Enos Slaughter (who led the team in most everything) and center-field magician Terry Moore were All-Stars, and 21-year-old Stan Musial was about to be. Not one pitcher who started a game compiled an ERA higher than 3.29. League MVP Mort Cooper's was 1.78, with 10 of his 22 wins coming via shutouts. Young Johnny Beazley went 21–6 and posted the league's second-lowest ERA (2.13). Their battery mate was Mort's brother Walker, the closest personality the Birds had to a Gashouser and reputed to be baseball's strongest man.

On August 4, St. Louis sported a 62–39 record but was 10 games behind the Dodgers, and this season seemed destined to be yet another near miss since the Cards won the 1934 title. Less than six weeks later, however, both clubs stood at 94–46. With 43 wins in their last 51 games—including 9 in their final 10—the Cards inched ahead for good to secure the pennant. Their 106 victories, still a franchise record, were the most by a National League team in 33 years.

As the season of dizzy achievement drew to a close, there was but one storm gathering in the distance: Branch Rickey was disgruntled.

The 1942 Cardinals were more than the sum of their parts. No batter hit .320, reached 15 homers, or drove in 100 runs.

This 1942 score card was sold to fans during Musial's first full season in the major leagues, when he turned in a solid year, hitting .315 with 10 homers and 72 RBI. His contributions helped the Cardinals to a franchise-record 106 wins and the first of three consecutive pennants.

Cards, Beazley Breeze Past Yankees

On the eve of the 1942 World Series, five of the previous six world-championship flags were flying above Yankee Stadium. To a team with a quintet of future Hall of Famers, St. Louis seemed like a minor obstacle on the way to another title. The Cardinals claimed to be unfazed, but they played horrifically in the opener, spotting the Yanks seven runs, going hitless until the eighth inning, and committing four errors. Even so, after flirting with a miracle rally in the ninth, "We couldn't wait to get back out on the field," claimed pitcher Ernie White. When they did, it was a different Cardinals ballclub.

Johnny Beazley blanked the Yanks for seven innings in Game 2, coughed up the lead, then was saved by Musial's RBI single and a bullet-throw from right fielder Enos Slaughter to nab a runner at third base. Moving to New York for Game 3, each St. Louis outfielder made a spectacular catch to preserve White's gritty shutout in the Bronx. Curveballing Max Lanier was the hero of the seesaw fourth game, restoring order with three scoreless relief innings as the Cards prevailed, 9–6.

To clinch by winning three straight at the Yankees' "house" was unthinkable, but two rookies—neither named Musial—thought otherwise.

Beazley made certain his last hurrah was a loud one. A month later, the right-hander would enlist in the Army, where he would hurt his arm and ruin his career,

but on this day he was a civilian hero. He limited the Yankees to two runs, matched by his teammates into the ninth. Then it was Whitey Kurowski's turn. The unheralded third baseman ripped a two-run homer, and St. Louis held on, 4–2.

When it was over, there was cheerfulness in the clubhouse, but neither champagne nor celebration. The 1942 Cardinals simply shook hands and went home, stoic champions.

Right: Third baseman Whitey Kurowski helped secure a shutout with this off-balance catch in the ninth inning of Game 3 of the 1942 World Series, but his true moment of heroism would come 48 hours later: a tiebreaking two-run homer in the top of the ninth of the clincher.

Yankees Take the Rematch

Such was the depth of Branch Rickey's farm system that the Cardinals of 1943 cakewalked to the pennant by 18 games even though ten players from the defending champs were called to World War II service for all or part of the season. And there was one other notable absence: Rickey himself, who left for the Dodgers when he and Sam Breadon could no longer stand each other.

The Yankees, though similarly depleted, were similarly dominant. Three of their Hall of Famers had swapped baseball threads for military uniforms, but manager Joe McCarthy's club was bent on retribution.

Perhaps it was a good omen for the "Bronx Bombers" during the World Series opener when a loud and fearsome B-17 inexplicably swooped over Yankee Stadium several times, the last within disconcerting proximity to the crowd. New York was a 4–2 winner. Max Lanier pitched well, but the Cardinals bats dozed into what would become an all-out coma.

The next day produced a win for the Cards—and a loss. The Cooper brothers got word before the game that their father had died, but Mort gutted out a complete game in a 4–3 Series-knotter. Four errors gifted the Yankees a 6–2 come-from-behind victory in the third game, so though the Cardinals were heading back home, their pulse was faint. Indeed, they would muster only one run in the final two meetings, wasting gems from Lanier and Cooper.

"We didn't have the intensity, the desire to win like we had in '42," recollected shortstop Marty Marion. "It was a war year. I don't think our minds were on it . . . but that was a poor excuse."

Above: A Marty Marion double scored Walker Cooper, but trailing runner Danny Litwhiler was out easily on a peg from Yankees right fielder Tuck Stainback to catcher Bill Dickey in the second inning of the 1943 World Series opener.

Right: Nearly 70,000 fans gave the Yankees a home-field advantage in the 1943 fall classic.

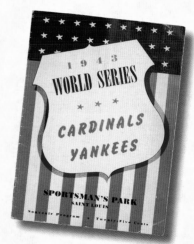

Above: For the second consecutive year and the fourth time in Cardinals history, the team found the New York Yankees waiting as its opponent in the 1943 World Series.

48

The "Streetcar Series"

The St. Louis Browns handed the favored Cardinals a stunning defeat in the first game of the 1944 "Streetcar Series" at Sportsman's Park. Here, third baseman Mark Christman fields a grounder from the Birds' Danny Litwhiler.

MVP SHOCKER: MARION PREVAILS

When a player bats .267 with six homers, and his teammate is Stan Musial, an MVP Award is the furthest thing from his mind. And so it was for Marty Marion in 1944. "I didn't [even] know what the hell it was," said the lanky shortstop. "Back then, it didn't mean a thing to me."

Conversely, Marion meant everything to the Cardinals. His defensive genius on a notoriously capricious Sportsman's Park infield was miraculous—and essential to a team that played a lot of low-scoring games. An inspired vote made Marty—christened "Slats" for his bed-slat-thin legs and "Octopus" for his long arms and suction-cup hands—the first shortstop to win the MVP as voted by the Baseball Writers' Association of America.

In 1944, manager Billy Southworth was still scratching for runs and still trampling the competition with pitching and defense. The season's outcome was never in doubt as the Cardinals became the first, and still only, team to win at least 105 games for a third consecutive year. But a routine pennant romp concluded with a twist: Their World Series foe would be the St. Louis Browns.

In the so-called "Streetcar Series," oddsmakers favored the Cards 2–1 over the upstart Browns, who were fresh off their lone pennant during their 52 seasons in St. Louis. To the surprise of the players, the city rallied behind them, which inspired the Browns at the beginning of the Series.

The first two games were washes, the Browns needing only two hits for a 2–1 victory in the opener and the Cards needing 11 innings to shake them in the rematch. After getting thumped 6–2 in Game 3, the Birds took nothing further for granted. Stan Musial heated up, Marty Marion's glovework astounded, rookie Emil Verban went 7-for-17 during the Series, Mort Cooper spun a dozen-strikeout shutout, and the Cardinals swept the next three games.

They could not have known that a baby named Anthony La Russa, Jr., had been born in Tampa, Florida, on October 4, the day the Series had begun.

These 1944 tickets to the Streetcar Series were hot items for baseball fans in St. Louis.

Soldiering on Through WWII

Like the attacks on the World Trade Center on September 11, 2001, the bombing of Pearl Harbor by the Japanese Navy on December 7, 1941, was a generation-defining event whose effects reverberated in every cranny of American life. Within days, war was declared on Japan and Germany, and baseball was not spared from the impact. In his "Green Light Letter," President Franklin D. Roosevelt gave the game his blessing to continue, citing its positive impact on the morale of the citizenry. The sport specifically asked for no special privileges in selective service practices or deployment. More than 500 major-leaguers served in the armed forces from 1942 to 1945, and rosters were

Frankie Frisch (center right) chats with Army Generals George S. Patton (center left) and Omar Bradley (left).

repopulated with second-liners and those with a disqualifying medical issue.

The redistribution of talent choked off dynasties and diluted the quality of play. Following the 1941 season, the Cardinals lost two players to the military. The next year it was ten, including such core operatives as Enos Slaughter, Terry Moore, and Johnny Beazley. Heading into 1944, nine more were gone—one of them Harry Walker, a Bronze Star and Purple Heart winner who served in General George Patton's Third Army. In 1945, the call to arms claimed seven more Birds, including stars Stan Musial, Max Lanier, and Walker Cooper.

The Cardinals, however, were in a better position than most to weather the attrition. The farm system was in peak production—an

The end of World War II brought several Cardinals back to the ballpark in 1946, including Enos Slaughter, who exchanged his army boots for baseball spikes and led the world champs with 130 RBI.

perceptibly when *balata*, a material recycled from golf ball covers, replaced rubber (needed for the war effort) in the manufacturing of baseballs. The result was something of a new dead-ball era, which played to the strengths of a contact-hitting, bat-handling, leather-flashing grinder such as "Slats."

Branch Rickey even had an antidote to the domino effect in his minor leagues. In the winter of 1943, he took out an ad in *The Sporting News* soliciting players. It read: "If you are now a free agent and have previous professional experience, we may be able to place you to your advantage on one of our clubs." About 250 farm teams were forced to disband during the war, but the Cardinals system soldiered fruitfully on.

A half-century later, President Bill Clinton—a lifelong Cardinals fan—addressed the nation in his weekly radio speech, hailing the return of the World Series after its 1994 hiatus. In it, he cited FDR's plea to let the games go on and affirmed that baseball teaches Americans to tolerate differences. "Everybody in the Midwest knows that when Cubs fans and Cardinals fans can sit down together," he added, "that's *real* tolerance." A labor dispute may have shut down the game during the Clinton administration, but World War II could not. Baseball, said Cards All-Star Enos Slaughter, an Army Air Corps veteran, "kept the spirit of the people up, and their minds off the war. I think it made everything go a little better."

The 1944 Redbirds became the third Cardinal team in as many years to win more than 100 games and claim the National League pennant. The difference this season was their opponent in the World Series: the Browns, making it an all-St. Louis World Series.

assembly line of talent. Walker came up when Slaughter and Moore departed, then Red Schoendienst buttressed a depleted outfield before developing into a Hall of Fame second baseman. Rookie Ken Burkhart won 18 games the year Lanier left. Howie Krist, a factor neither before nor after the war, went 34–8 during it. The team also profited from a bittersweet blessing: One of Marty Marion's legs was shorter than the other as a result of a childhood accident, keeping him out of the service but eventually shortening his career.

A player of Marion's ilk was especially precious in these years. The game changed

A "Floating Ghost" at Shortstop

Marty Marion is the only eighth-place hitter ever to win an MVP Award, which he did by a single vote in 1944 thanks to his glittering glovework, slick bat-handling, and mature leadership.

SUPPORT FOR HIS BRETHREN

In an era when ballplayers bordered on indentured servitude, Marion was a fiscal sophisticate. Once, he prevented Branch Rickey from releasing his brother Red by producing an old envelope on which he had taken notes (at age 17!) from a meeting in which the team president had promised both a four-year trial.

In the mid-1940s, Marty was at the vanguard of one of the earliest attempts by players to unionize. Though owners quashed the endeavor, he eventually convinced them to establish the game's first pension plan.

From 1940 through 1950, the Cardinals won more games (1,038) and, with the help of their vacuumlike defense, compiled the lowest ERA (3.26) of any team in baseball. Their shortstop in those years never hit higher than .280 or even reached double digits in home runs or stolen bases. But between 1919 (when Rogers Hornsby moved to third base before switching to second base) and the arrival of Ozzie Smith in 1982, Marty Marion was the class of the Cardinals at the position. Leadership, flawless fundamentals, and especially his glove made him so.

"Thank you, Marty, thank you," Whitey Kurowski would mutter, glove in front of his lips, when Marion would get to a ball that the rigid third baseman couldn't reach. The appreciation extended to awards by voters who made "Slats" an All-Star on eight occasions and the 1944 National League MVP. Standing 6'2" in an era when shortstops were almost exclusively "smurfs," the savvy South Carolinian conceded nothing in sheer athletic grace. The great Yankee catcher Bill Dickey once referred to him as "a regular floating ghost."

Back problems ended Marion's career in his early 30s, but he managed the Cardinals in 1951. Long after his playing days, he found another way to serve the club and its fans: as manager and part-owner of the Stadium Club at Busch for 18 years.

The Cooper Brothers

They neither looked alike nor acted alike, but for three years battery mates Morton and Walker Cooper were inseparable sibling superstars. On the Cardinals' pennant-winning clubs of 1942, 1943, and 1944, they were the elite at their positions. On the mound, the elder "Mort" won 65 games, with 23 shutouts and an ERA of 2.17—all tops in the game. Meanwhile, "Walk" batted .305 with 132 extra-base hits and 218 RBI—baseball's best among catchers.

While both often performed at a Hall of Fame level, many factors collaborated to frustrate the Coopers' careers. Neither even played their first big-league game until they were 25. Dark-haired, prickly Mort labored in pain much of the time from the bone chips in his elbow. The blond and subtly mischievous Walk made a more cogent case for immortality with eight All-Star Game selections. However, he lost a prime season to military service and, though he was still a dangerous hitter into the 1950s, by then he had long since exhausted his defensive agility.

Neither Mort's stint with the Cardinals nor his life itself ended well. In 1945, he went AWOL from the team in a salary dispute and was tersely traded. After that, he was a shadow of his former self on account of his injury. He died of a lung condition at 45.

Mort's brother made St. Louis regret selling him to the Giants in 1946. Walk hit 35 home runs in 1947, which was the second highest homer tally ever for a catcher at the time. In 1949, he was the first backstop to have a 10-RBI game. He also became the first player ever to hit grand slams with five different teams. After the 1957 season, he finally realized it was time to retire when his daughter married his teammate, second baseman Don Blasingame.

As teammates for seven seasons (six with the Cardinals), catcher Walker (left) and pitcher Mort Cooper formed the longest-running brother battery in baseball history. They were also the starting NL tandem in the 1942 and 1943 All-Star Games.

Pitcher Morton Cooper led the National League with 22 wins and a 1.78 ERA in 1942 and was named the league's Most Valuable Player. The only other Cardinal pitchers ever to be named MVP are Dizzy Dean and Bob Gibson.

MORTON COOPER

BY 1944, WINNING THE PENNANT HAD BECOME A REGULAR OCCURRENCE FOR THE CARDINALS, BUT NOBODY IN ST. LOUIS WAS COMPLAINING.

Sportsman's Park, St. Louis, Missouri

SPORTSMAN'S PARK, ON THE CORNER OF GRAND AND DODIER IN ST. LOUIS, WAS THE HOME FOR BOTH THE CARDINALS AND BROWNS FROM 1920 UNTIL 1953, WHEN THE BROWNS MOVED TO BALTIMORE AND BECAME THE ORIOLES. THE STADIUM WAS RENAMED BUSCH STADIUM WHEN AUGUST A. BUSCH, JR., BOUGHT THE CARDINALS THAT SAME YEAR.

THE CARDINALS LOGO HAS ALWAYS BEEN ONE OF THE MOST POPULAR IN SPORTS, AND IT IS OFTEN FEATURED ON UNIQUE ITEMS, SUCH AS THIS ASHTRAY.

IN 1944, SHORTSTOP MARTY MARION BECAME THE FIRST PLAYER TO RECEIVE THE MVP AWARD BASICALLY FOR HIS DEFENSIVE ABILITY. HE WON THE HONOR EVEN THOUGH FIVE PLAYERS ON HIS OWN TEAM HIT FOR A HIGHER AVERAGE, SIX HAD MORE RBI, AND SIX HIT MORE HOME RUNS. HERE IS HIS SPECIAL GLOVE.

THE CARDINALS AND YANKEES WERE TIED AT ONE WIN EACH IN THE 1942 WORLD SERIES WHEN THE SERIES SHIFTED TO NEW YORK FOR THE NEXT THREE GAMES. A 2-0 WIN PUT THE CARDINALS AHEAD TO STAY AS THEY WON THE NEXT TWO CONTESTS TO CLOSE OUT THE SERIES IN FIVE GAMES.

LIGHTS WERE INSTALLED AT SPORTSMAN'S PARK IN 1940. THE BROWNS PLAYED A NIGHT GAME IN THE STADIUM FIRST, WITH THE CARDINALS' FIRST HOME GAME COMING ON JUNE 4, 1940, WHEN THEY LOST 10-1 TO BROOKLYN.

THE CARDINALS WERE HAPPY TO PLAY ANYBODY OTHER THAN THE YANKEES IN THE 1944 WORLD SERIES, BUT THEY WERE EVEN HAPPIER THAT THE ST. LOUIS BROWNS WON THE AL PENNANT, WHICH MEANT NO TRAVEL, WITH EVERY GAME BEING PLAYED IN SPORTSMAN'S PARK. THE CARDINALS WON THE SERIES IN SIX GAMES.

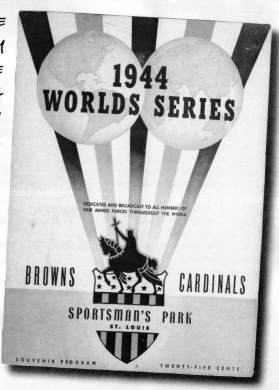

Slaughter's Mad Dash

As the 1946 campaign loomed, the Cardinals were "stuck" with an embarrassment of riches. A team that had averaged 103 wins the previous four years welcomed back 22 players from World War II service. Owner Sam Breadon saw this not as depth, but dollar signs. He lined his pockets with the proceeds of numerous player sales, calculating that he still would have plenty of horses to win another pennant. His handicapping proved accurate, but only by a nose.

Back from the military were Stan Musial (who would be the NL's 1946 MVP), Enos Slaughter (its RBI champ), Harry Walker (one year shy of a batting title), and Howie Pollet (the new 21-game-winning ace). Gifted young reinforcements included second baseman Red Schoendienst and catcher Joe Garagiola. Such was the saturation of Rickey-ripened talent throughout the league that nearly half the players on its All-Star team were current or former Cardinals.

Yet the season was a rocky one for rookie manager Eddie Dyer. The Birds found themselves depleted by injuries and distracted by a money-waving raid from the Mexican League that claimed three players and tempted even Musial. When it ended, the Cardinals were in a dead heat with the Dodgers. That set up the first playoff (best out of three) in major-league history. St. Louis quickly won twice and advanced to the World Series against the Boston Red Sox. As with the regular season, the outcome was not assured until the final pitch.

The Cardinals blew a 2–1 ninth-inning lead in the Series opener and succumbed in

In the 1946 World Series against the Boston Red Sox, manager Eddie Dyer employed the "Williams Shift," swinging his infielders drastically toward right field. Ted walked in this at-bat in the opener and would hit only .200 for the Series.

Nothing came easy for the 1946 Cards, as they needed to win a National League playoff and then seven World Series games (climaxed by a one-run heart-stopper) to secure the championship.

In 2003, *Time* magazine slotted this No. 9 on its list of "Ten Indelible Images from the Fall Classic." Enos Slaughter's "Mad Dash" to score the winning run of the 1946 World Series is No. 1 to Cardinals fans.

tying two-run double. In the bottom half, Slaughter led off with a single and still stood at first two outs later. Then came the most famous sprint in Cardinals history.

Walker ripped a pitch to left-center for a hit, and Slaughter never stopped running. By the time Boston's relay man, Johnny Pesky, turned, Enos had raced through a stop sign and was steaming toward home. A shocked Pesky hesitated just an instant, and his throw was too late to shoot down the go-ahead run. Brecheen escaped a ninth-inning jam, and Slaughter's "Mad Dash" became one of the classic moments in the annals of baseball. The Cardinals had their sixth title in 21 years. And, for quite some time, their last.

Enos Slaughter was not known for his defensive skills (shown is his glove), but the 1946 Cardinals outfield of Slaughter, Terry Moore, and Harry Walker was as good as there was in baseball that year.

the tenth. With the Cards' hitting slump obviously carrying over from September, they needed a shut-down pitching performance. They got one from Harry Brecheen. "The Cat" blanked the BoSox on four hits. Boston's Boo Ferriss responded in kind, 4–0, in Game 3. Then the bats finally combusted, the Cards tying a Series record with 20 hits (including four apiece by Enos Slaughter, Whitey Kurowski, and Joe Garagiola) in a 12–3 laugher. Back and forth it went the next two games: a 6–3 Boston win followed by another Brecheen gem, 4–1.

The 36,143 fans on hand in St. Louis for the deciding game were gloriously tortured. The Cardinals led 3–1 in the eighth inning until "The Cat" nearly became a goat when he came out of the bullpen to surrender a

A MILLION STRONG

Giddy from victory in World War II and starved for recreational release, Americans herded to baseball games in the late 1940s. And so they did in St. Louis, where, in 1946, Cardinals attendance nearly doubled from the previous year and surpassed one million (1,062,553) for the first time. The next season, the draw swelled to 1,248,013, then in 1949 to 1,430,676—a team record until 1966, when the 50,000-seat Busch Memorial Stadium made its debut.

America put on a fresher, happier face when the boys came home from World War II, and baseball played a cathartic role in the nation's emotional resuscitation. These young fans at Sportsman's Park cheered on a Cardinals victory in Game 6 of the 1946 World Series.

Hitchhiking to Cooperstown

Red Schoendienst first leaped into Cardinals lore as an acrobatic second baseman who developed into a .300 hitter and then a highly successful manager. In 1950, he hit a 14th-inning home run to win the All-Star Game.

Red Schoendienst was always something different—and better—than he was thought to be.

He wasn't supposed to be army-eligible because of an eye injury, but he talked his way in. He might never have been discovered, had he not hitchhiked from Illinois to Missouri with 50 cents in his pocket for a baseball audition. He didn't look like a ballplayer. In fact, his first minor-league manager, Pepper Martin, saw his frailty and freckles and mistook him for a batboy. He was a pure infielder, but he took one for the team by moonlighting as an outfielder as a 1945 rookie. In the 1950s, he shouldn't have been ambulatory, but he still played with pleurisy and myriad injuries. Late in his career, he might have died but made a comeback after he'd lost part of a lung to tuberculosis. Even his early Topps baseball cards called him the unfamiliar "Al."

Schoendienst's tenacity made him one of the greatest defensive stars in history. He topped league second basemen in fielding percentage seven times, and he is still the Cardinals' career record-holder for the position in that stat (.983), assists (4,130), putouts (3,684), and double plays (1,092). He was smart and pesky at the plate, where he batted .289, with nearly 600 extra-base hits. From 1946 to 1957, he made 10 of the 12 All-Star teams. Schoendienst's leadership qualities then translated seamlessly to the manager's seat, as he skippered the Cardinals to 1,041 wins and the 1967 World Series title.

Many years later, Red reflected on the lift he got to his tryout: "I never thought that milk truck ride would eventually lead to Cooperstown."

Five players who appeared in a Cardinals uniform in the 1940s have been selected for the Hall of Fame in Cooperstown, including Red Schoendienst, who is pictured in this inaugural 1952 Topps card.

Bleeding Cardinal Red

Every day on a diamond was a "Mad Dash" for Enos Slaughter. It started one afternoon when Eddie Dyer, his manager at Class-B Columbus, chastised him for not hustling. From then on, Slaughter never stopped hustling. For "Country," a walk meant a run to first base. Every return to his outfield post was a full sprint.

Determined to make the 1939 team, Slaughter reported to spring training even though he had a debilitating case of rabbit fever that had killed his father just weeks before. He went on to hit .320 that season. In 1941, he played with a broken collar bone, once swinging so hard at a pitch that blood spurted from the wound. After returning from a three-year service stint, his daring baserunning and clutch hitting won the 1946 World Series for St. Louis, though few recall he played the last three games with a broken elbow that soon developed a blood clot. ("The fellers need me," he explained.) At age 40 with the Yankees, Slaughter was reportedly timed at a swift 3.6 seconds from home to first. At 43, he pinch-hit with a broken foot.

The cannon-armed Hall of Famer was an All-Star in 10 of his 13 seasons with St. Louis. He hit an even .300 for his career, augmenting that with the third-highest sums of walks and triples in franchise history.

Above all, Enos bled Cardinal red. When he was traded to the Yankees in 1954, he equated his grief to the day his father died. But he never stopped hustling. "When I played ball, regardless of what uniform I wore," he said, "I gave them 100 percent."

Finally being able to add "Hall of Fame" to his biography was a major moment in Enos Slaughter's life.

WILMER MIZELL NEVER WON MORE THAN 14 GAMES IN HIS SEVEN SEASONS WITH THE CARDINALS IN THE 1950S AND 1960, BUT HE DID POSSESS ONE OF THE BEST NICKNAMES OF ALL TIME: "VINEGAR BEND." THAT NICKNAME WAS IN HONOR OF HIS HOMETOWN OF VINEGAR BEND, ALABAMA.

THE CARDINALS FINISHED A DISAPPOINTING SEVENTH IN 1955, BUT HOPES FOR IMPROVEMENT IN THE FUTURE WERE TRIGGERED BY THE ARRIVAL OF TWO ROOKIES: OUTFIELDER BILL VIRDON (THE NL ROOKIE OF THE YEAR) AND THIRD BASEMAN KEN BOYER. VIRDON'S STAY IN ST. LOUIS WAS BRIEF; HE WAS TRADED TO PITTSBURGH A YEAR LATER.

IN HIS CAREER, KEN BOYER WON FIVE GOLD GLOVES FOR FIELDING EXCELLENCE AS A THIRD BASEMAN. HE ALSO WAS THE NL MVP IN 1964 AFTER LEADING THE CARDINALS TO THEIR FIRST PENNANT IN 18 YEARS. HIS GRAND SLAM IN GAME 4 OF THE WORLD SERIES AGAINST THE YANKEES WAS THE TURNING POINT IN THE CARDINALS' EVENTUAL VICTORY.

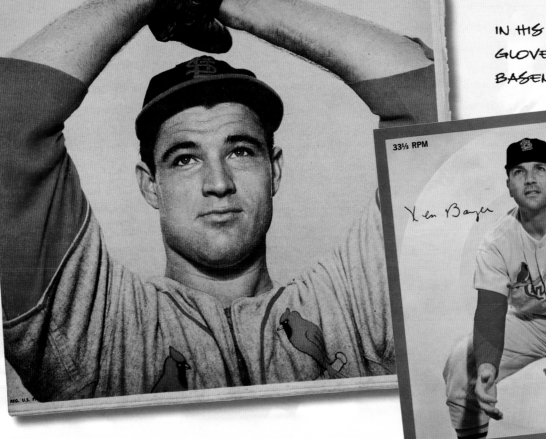

THE ST. LOUIS
Cardinals
1955   50c

parade
ST. LOUIS POST-DISPATCH

THE SHOCKING TRUTH ABOUT
WHY KIDS QUIT SCHOOL
PAGE 8

April 1

WILMER (VINEGAR BEND) MIZELL:
The St. Louis Cardinals' hope . . . page 10

33⅓ RPM

SPORTS RECORD

Ken Boyer

REG. U.S.

THE CARDINALS HOSTED THE ANNUAL ALL-STAR GAME FOR THE THIRD TIME IN 1957. THE AMERICAN LEAGUE WON 6-5, SCORING THREE RUNS IN THE TOP OF THE NINTH AND THEN HOLDING OFF AN NL RALLY IN THE BOTTOM OF THE INNING. MINNIE MINOSO CAUGHT GIL HODGES'S LINE DRIVE WITH A RUNNER ON AND TWO OUTS TO END THE THREE-RUN RALLY AND THE GAME.

BASEBALL WAS STILL A BARGAIN IN 1956: RESERVED SEATS AT BUSCH STADIUM COST $1.85, AND CHILDREN UNDER 12 COULD BUY A TICKET FOR $1.25.

DURING BOTH HIS PLAYING AND MANAGING CAREER, RED SCHOENDIENST WAS ALWAYS WILLING TO ACCOMODATE FANS WHO WANTED HIS AUTOGRAPH.

EXCEPT FOR THE PERFORMANCE OF STAN MUSIAL, THE 1950S WAS NOT A GREAT DECADE FOR THE CARDINALS. THEY FINISHED HIGHER THAN THIRD IN THE NL ONLY ONCE—A SECOND-PLACE FINISH IN 1957, EIGHT GAMES BEHIND THE PENNANT-WINNING MILWAUKEE BRAVES.

Busch Rules for 37 Years

In 1947, a cancer-stricken Sam Breadon, the Cardinals owner of 27 years, sold the franchise to—of all people—a Cubs fan. But Fred Saigh came to love his team, and it was with a heavy heart that he decided to divest himself of the team six years later following his conviction on what appeared to be a trumped-up charge of tax evasion. For months, it was far from certain that the city of St. Louis could retain its beloved team. Enter August Busch, Jr.—almost literally on a white horse.

Architect of the rise of St. Louis-based Anheuser-Busch into the world's largest brewery, "Gussie" got his start sweeping floors for the family business. He obviously knew how to succeed, and he also knew how to make an entrance, delighting the city when his company purchased the ballclub and, later,

by riding regally into the park behind his famous team of immense Clydesdale horses.

Busch was what announcer Harry Caray called a "booze and broads" man. Though not always a prudent decision-maker, nor even an enthusiastic fan at first, he eventually became a celebrated baseball man. While the club endured phases of frustration and folly under his 37-year stewardship, milestones were established with the purchase of one ballpark and the building of a spectacular new one. During this era the Cardinals captured six NL pennants and three World Series titles, all the while selling few tickets and struggling with poor attendance.

In 1984, the uniform number 85 (Busch's age at the time) was retired, and in 2007 his name was added to the Hall of Fame Veteran's Committee ballot. Each year, Major League Baseball presents the August A. Busch Award to an individual for long and meritorious service to the game.

Before August A. Busch, Jr., stepped forward and had Anheuser Busch buy the Cardinals from Fred Saigh in 1953, it appeared the Browns would be the team staying in St. Louis and that the Cardinals would be sold and moved to Milwaukee.

Gussie Busch (center) wore the pants in the Cardinals family as the club owner from 1 1953 to 1989. Here he meets with several of his new employees—from left, manager Eddie Stanky, Enos Slaughter, Red Schoendienst, and Stan Musial—for the first time during spring training.

Redbirds Almost Fly Away

By the 1950s, the Cardinals were a local treasure. The team had been a bridesmaid since winning it all in 1946, but it was part of the constitution of St. Louis, attendance consistently twice what it was before the war. Fred Saigh's announcement that the club was for sale was a haymaker in the city's gut. And the bellyache worsened when it became apparent that no one in the St. Louis area was interested in purchasing it. Saigh had no choice but to consider offers from interests in Houston and Milwaukee.

What happened next and why is a matter of contention. Conventional wisdom hails Gussie Busch as the man who saved the Cardinals. According to Saigh, that may be only technically true. Busch, he contended, wanted no part of the team and should not be regarded by history as a savior. Only after some persuasion by local businessmen and a sweet financial deal, he claimed, did Busch bite. But in a momentous act of civic duty, Saigh agreed to accept $3.75 million—appreciably less than he would have gotten from out-of-town suitors—from the beer baron. His sacrifice intercepted a civic cataclysm and set the stage for an ongoing half-century-plus of dynamic Cards baseball.

The gambit was a death knell for the Browns, already far inferior in resources and results. In 1954, facing receivership, they moved to Baltimore and were renamed the Orioles. For the first time since 1901, St. Louis was a one-team town.

BUDWEISER STADIUM

His acquisition complete, Gussie Busch moved swiftly to purchase dilapidated Sportsman's Park from the Browns. His intention to christen it Budweiser Stadium, however, was met with indignation by temperance groups and several league owners. So Gussie relented and named it after his family. Within two years, he had spent nearly half the cost of the club itself to renovate Busch Stadium. That price tag included a refurbishing of the left-field scoreboard—complete with a giant Budweiser sign.

Sportsman's Park in the 1940s was more about tradition and a crusty sort of charm than aesthetics. Cardinals attendance was typically middle-of-the-pack in the National League throughout its service.

Alston Breaks the Barrier

New owner Gussie Busch looked around at his team's 1953 spring training lineup and frankly addressed his coaches: "Where are our black players?" Told there were none, his reply plotted the course for the Cardinals to integrate, however belatedly: "How can it be the great American game if blacks can't play?"

In 1954, seven years after Jackie Robinson ruptured the color barrier, Busch made his team the tenth of the game's 16 franchises to integrate by acquiring both the black man he wanted and the first baseman he needed: Tom Alston of the Triple-A San Diego Padres. (Len Tucker was the first African-American to sign with St. Louis, but he never made the majors.)

Alston seemed to be a solid prospect. He stood 6′5″, weighed 210 pounds, ran

well, and was coming off a season in which he'd pounded 23 home runs. Unfortunately, the lefty-hitting North Carolinian seemed ill-equipped to handle the pressure of his mission or the inside fastball. Beset by a mysterious illness and perhaps paralyzed by expectations, he batted only .246 in 66 games that season and would play only sparingly for three years afterward.

Pitcher Brooks Lawrence, who joined the team in June 1954 as its second African-American, said he would hear his roommate praying in the middle of the night, repeating, "I can hit. I *know* I can hit." But Alston never did, and he evidently began to unravel. After he quit playing, he admitted to a church arson and spent a decade in a mental institution.

Long after his retirement, Alston's story was recounted by singer-songwriter Bruce Piephoff in the song, "Big Foot in the Door": *"I seen him yesterday at the Woolworth store... eating meals alone."*

A tall, gangly first baseman, Tom Alston became the first black player in Cardinals history in 1954. A good Triple-A player, Alston never matched that success and lasted just parts of four seasons in St. Louis, playing a total of only 91 games.

The Cardinals were disappointed that their first black player, Tom Alston, did not enjoy greater success in his major-league career.

From Billy the Kid to Stone Face

Far left: By many criteria, Billy Southworth was the best manager the franchise has ever had. During the war years, "The Little General" won three pennants, two World Series, and almost two thirds of his games.

Left center: Eddie Dyer, here engaged in a nail-biter with the Cubs in 1949, presided over the last gasp of what could be characterized as a quarter-century-long dynasty. He won a WS title as a rookie skipper, then finished second three straight years.

In the middle of the 1929 season, owner Sam Breadon banished the most successful manager in the history of the franchise to a minor-league assignment; he just didn't know it yet. Back then, Billy Southworth was caught between two worlds—a player-manager whom his players considered an uppity taskmaster. Eleven years later, he returned well-seasoned and reborn as a patient, empathetic leader. Starting with his takeover from Ray Blades in June 1940, "Billy the Kid" won nearly two thirds of his regular-season games, three pennants, and two World Series before the Boston Braves hired him in 1946.

His surprise successor, Eddie Dyer, was formerly a successful minor-league skipper and the team's farm director. He inherited a dugout teeming with talent, then used it deftly to show the baseball world that the Cardinals were not merely a wartime

phenomenon by becoming only the second rookie manager in history to win a World Series. Dyer resigned after a substandard 1950 season but, in between, steered three second-place teams.

Marty Marion lasted just one so-so season as Dyer's replacement and then was fired in favor of Eddie Stanky, who was acquired from the Giants to be the Cards' player-manager in 1952. Although the brash, brusque "Brat" boasted a superior baseball mind, most of his players loathed him. "The Cards," said Enos Slaughter, "were all fine people, except one. That was Eddie Stanky." Middle-of-the-pack results got him sacked in 1955.

The 1956 season brought Fred Hutchinson, whose nickname "Stone Face" belied his propensity for furniture-throwing temper tantrums. Hutch sandwiched a 1957 Manager of the Year Award in between a couple of sub-.500 seasons before he was dismissed.

Right center: Eddie Stanky's over-the-top competitiveness didn't translate especially well to managerial duties in the mid-1950s. As a second baseman, he hatched the now-illegal "Stanky Maneuver" in which he'd jump up and down and wave his arms to distract batters.

Far right: Only moderately effective in his three seasons as manager in St. Louis, Fred Hutchinson later had success with the Reds before succumbing to cancer at age 45. Each year, baseball presents the Hutch Award to a player who exemplifies his competitive spirit.

The Men at the Mic

For a generation of St. Louis Cardinals fans, summer had two voices and one radio address. From 1955 until 1969, the men behind the Cardinals mic—one a kid from St. Louis who dreamed of playing for the Cards and the other raised in Massachusetts and educated at Ohio State—shared the booth at KMOX. And for the fans that heard them, Harry Caray and Jack Buck remain the paradigm against which all other broadcasters are judged.

Caray was born Harry Carabina in St. Louis and grew up in Webster Groves, Missouri, as a die-hard Birds fan and a fine youth baseball player. When his diamond dreams didn't pan out, he climbed through the minors as a broadcaster before reaching the major leagues in 1945. An immediate hit with fans, Caray was often less popular with players and (especially) managers because of

Jack Buck, Caray's successor as the lead radio play-by-play man, was a "winner" as a professional and as a respected personality. At Busch Stadium in 1998, the club unveiled a bronze bust of their long-time "voice," smiling behind a microphone, with a hand cupped over his ear.

Little did Harry Caray know that, when this 1969 photo was taken, it would depict his final game behind the Cardinals mike. His "Holy Cow!" (an expression he trained himself to use to avoid profanity) had punctuated St. Louis airwaves for a quarter-century.

his tendency to speak his mind. "I fired him about three times," former Cardinals owner Fred Saigh told author Peter Golenbock. "Harry was a great second-guesser, and our manager, Eddie Dyer, would come to me and threaten 'either Caray or me!' So I'd fire Caray for a day or two, and they'd kiss and make up, and we'd hire him back."

Though beloved by listeners, his partners—everyone from Gabby Street to Joe Garagiola—came and went, unable to find a rhythm with the spotlight-stealing Caray. Then the low-key Buck, in his first big-league broadcasting gig, arrived. The World War II Purple Heart winner would one day succeed Caray as the Cards lead announcer and reign for three decades, but he was not yet 30 when he parked next to Caray and proved an ideal foil.

> "THERE WAS NO DOUBT IN MY MIND," HE SAID, "THAT ... WITH MY LAST GASP I'D SAY, 'CARDINALS WIN!'"
> —HARRY CARAY

Cardinal Nation was in mourning twice in a five-day period in 2002, first with the death of legendary broadcaster Jack Buck after a long illness and then with the sudden death of Cards pitcher Darryl Kile, who was found dead in his Chicago hotel room while the Cardinals were playing the Cubs.

During their 16 years together, the two were a study in counterpoint. Buck simply told it genially and precisely like it was in his gravelly baritone, coining no phrase more colorful than "That's a winner!" Caray, however, was excitable and prone to repeated exclamations of "Holy cow!" and either exhorting or excoriating his team. "Sometimes he went too far trying to create and stir controversy," admitted Buck, "but he was talented as hell. And people anywhere, they liked his honesty."

Caray unfailingly handled the first and final thirds of each game, with Buck stepping in to do both color and play-by-play analysis during the fourth through sixth innings. "If a game went to extra innings, I might as well have gone home," Buck wrote in his autobiography,

"because Caray was going to do all the play-by-play. It upset him if he wasn't on the air when something exciting happened."

With KMOX's powerful signal reaching far beyond the St. Louis city limits, the two voices reared legions of Cardinals fans on both sides of the Mississippi. "Nobody had, I think, the kind of following Harry did when he was with the Cardinals," said Milo Hamilton, one of his former boothmates. "Nobody ever broadcast like he has. Nobody could if they wanted to."

That's why it was stunning when Caray was fired on vague grounds after the 1969 season. Even *he* was stopped cold by the announcement. "There was no doubt in my mind," he said, "that ... with my last gasp I'd say, 'Cardinals win!'"

Jack Buck (left) and Harry Caray first worked together calling Cardinal games on KXOK radio in 1954 before moving to KMOX a year later.

STAN MUSIAL'S 3,000TH CAREER HIT WAS HEADLINE NEWS IN THE ST. LOUIS POST-DISPATCH.

ONE OF THE MOST DISTINCTIVE ASPECTS OF STAN MUSIAL'S CAREER WAS HIS UNIQUE BATTING STANCE. HE SPRUNG FROM THAT STANCE TO ATTACK OPPOSING PITCHERS, FINISHING HIS CAREER WITH 3,630 HITS, THE MOST IN NL HISTORY WHEN HE RETIRED. EXACTLY HALF— 1,815—CAME AT HOME AND THE OTHER 1,815 CAME ON THE ROAD.

IN HONOR OF HIS 3,000TH CAREER HIT, A PINCH-HIT DOUBLE OFF THE CUBS' MOE DRABOWSKY AT WRIGLEY FIELD ON MAY 13, 1958, MUSIAL RECEIVED A PAIR OF CUSTOM-MADE CUFF LINKS AND A TIE TACK MADE OF 14 CARAT GOLD.

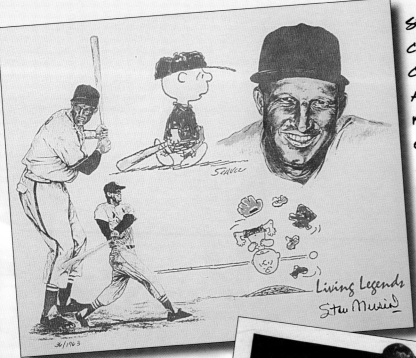

Living Legends
Stan Musial

STAN MUSIAL COUNTED MANY CELEBRITIES AMONG HIS CLOSE PERSONAL FRIENDS. ONE OF THEM, CHARLES SCHULZ, THE CREATOR OF THE *PEANUTS* COMIC STRIP, DEPICTED MUSIAL AND CHARLIE BROWN IN THIS DRAWING.

STAN "THE MAN" MUSIAL WAS SO POPULAR THAT HE COULD HAVE RUN FOR PRESIDENT OR AT LEAST GOVERNOR OF MISSOURI. HE WAS A GUEST OF MANY PRESIDENTS AT THE WHITE HOUSE, AND HIS 22 SEASONS AS A CARDINAL SET A RECORD WHICH MAY NEVER BE BROKEN.

MUSIAL WAS A POPULAR PITCHMAN FOR MANY COMPANIES IN THE 1950S, INCLUDING WHEATIES CEREAL. THIS AD APPEARED ON THE BACK COVER OF DELL COMIC BOOKS.

Stan Musial shows son Dickie how to snag a wide one. St. Louis Cards' slugging outfielder hopes someday to see Dickie a champion too . . . belting homers . . . winning a case of Wheaties every time. Could be! This eight year old "rookie" has eaten Wheaties several years already.

Start them young if you want your youngster to develop the energy and endurance of true champions! See that they get like champions. Begin breakfast with that famous training dish—Wheaties, milk and fruit. Many big leaguers started eating these whole wheat flakes in childhood.

Champi... start you...

'48 batting champion Musial says, "I'd advise any young athlete to start on Wheaties. Swell for flavor . . . and nourishing." Many a top flight athletic coach agrees with Stan . . . likes Wheaties on the team's training table. Wheaties, with that second-helping flavor millions love! Had your Wheaties today?

"Wheaties" and "Breakfast of Champions" are registered trade marks of General Mills

JOIN THE CHAMPIONS . . . TOMORROW!

Does Dick eat more than dad? Ask Mom she knows! Speaking for himself, Stan Musial says, "You'll find me polishing off a couple of bowlfuls of Wheaties most every morning." Want to bet Dick keeps up? Real enjoyment for all the family in these 100% whole wheat flakes. He-man nourishment, too . . . three B vitamins, also minerals, food energy, proteins. Wheaties a year 'round training dish of many famous stars—Musial, Bauduon, Stephens, Lemon, Bearden. Have Wheaties tomorrow.

"Breakfast of Champions"

ON JUNE 22, 1962, MUSIAL PASSED ONE OF THE TRUE BASEBALL LEGENDS, TY COBB, WHEN HE COLLECTED THE 5,864TH TOTAL BASE OF HIS CAREER DURING A FOUR-HIT DAY THAT INCLUDED A HOME RUN IN A DOUBLEHEADER AGAINST THE PHILLIES AT CONNIE MACK STADIUM.

The Cardinals Experience

The efforts by new owner Gussie Busch to improve Busch Stadium made it a popular spot for St. Louisans and visitors in the 1950s.

When pitcher Max Lanier was first called up to the Cardinals in the late 1930s, he complained there was nothing to do after a game but get a root beer float and spit seeds at "Sal's watermelon place." By the time he was traded before the 1952 season, the city of St. Louis proper was bustling with an even greater population than it has today. And throughout the 1950s, there were few more appealing attractions to its residents than spending a day in and around Busch Stadium.

It wasn't that the locals weren't fond of the pre-Busch version of Sportsman's Park, the quintessential ugly

LET'S GO SEE THE
Cardinals

Bobblehead dolls didn't really become a novelty item until decades later, but the Cardinals had their own bobblehead doll in the 1950s.

beauty. St. Louis native and baseball historian William B. Mead called it "the most beautiful edifice ever built." He wrote that it "satisfied the senses" even though "the unswept grime crunched underfoot, and the park reeked of beer and other drippings." Marty Marion once referred to Sportsman's as "a little downtown crackerbox, but a great place to play." But when August Busch, Jr., bought it, renamed it, and hurriedly "gussied" it up, it was a brand new ballgame.

The stadium was repainted red, jade green, and metallic blue. New seats were installed; restrooms and concession stands were overhauled; even entrances, aisles, and ramps were given a facelift. The lighting system was upgraded, and the chewed-up playing surface was repaired. The center-field seats were replaced with shrubbery, an aesthetic improvement and a natural backdrop for batters. On top of the scoreboard in left-center, Busch installed a Budweiser eagle that would flap its wings after every home-team home run. And a bat-swinging cardinal would indicate whether a play was scored a hit or an error. Budweiser replaced Griesedieck as the official ballpark beer, of course. A bottle cost a quarter and was a refreshing chaser to a 15-cent hot dog. Bud also became the only brew served

across the street at Palermo's Tavern, a popular hangout beyond the left-field gate. Busch repaid proprietor Jimmy Palermo's loyalty by periodically popping into his establishment and buying a few rounds for the house. A favorite of fans and players alike, Palermo's was quite possibly America's first sports bar and just one of many unpretentious ballpark-area joints that bulged with folks before and after games.

By 1956, Palermo's even had a television installed over the bar. But for Cardinals fans, the best views were to be found across the street in the ballyard most St. Louisans continued to call Sportsman's Park. Tickets stayed in every family's price range throughout the decade, starting at 75 cents in the bleachers (free, of course, to kids holding a Knothole Gang Pass) and topping out at $2.25 for a box seat. The familiar, familial feeling in the stands, however, was priceless. So intimate was the experience that after bellowing encouragement from their seats, Cards-rooters routinely elicited postgame conversation and autographs from players met in the tunnel to the clubhouse, then open to fans.

Win or lose, even in a decade in which the team did similar numbers of both, Busch Stadium was the place to be on a St. Louis summer afternoon.

It was no surprise when Stan Musial's name headed the list of baseball's top batters at the end of the 1952 season—his third consecutive and sixth overall title.

CHAPTER FOUR

SIXTIES SENSATIONS
1960–1969

THE CARDINALS ENTERED the 1960s in a funk, but they came out the other end as one of the most successful franchises of the era. Only the Giants won more National League games in the decade, and St. Louis's three pennants and two world championships matched the Dodgers' output. Although Stan Musial and Sportsman's Park faded away, Bob Gibson and Busch Memorial Stadium not only safeguarded the Cardinal tradition, but they also fortified it.

Above: The Cardinals gave their fans plenty to cheer about in a short period of time in the 1960s, winning three pennants and two World Series titles from 1964 to 1968.

Right: In the gripping 1967 World Series, Bob Gibson strolled off the mound three times with complete games.

Right: Perhaps the most competitive pitcher in major-league history, Bob Gibson was at his best in big contests, such as this 1968 World Series game.

Captain Ken

Above: Ken Boyer, captain of the 1964 Cardinals, was named the NL MVP for leading the team to its first pennant in 18 years. He then delivered the key hit in the World Series against the Yankees, a grand slam off Al Downing in Game 4.

Right: Ken Boyer is among the most beloved Cardinals for his steady play, class, and leadership. He hit inside-the-park home runs in three consecutive weeks in May and June of 1959.

There is only one position at which no Cardinal who played after 1900 is enshrined in the Hall of Fame. That's third base, and any fan who saw Ken Boyer play that position will confirm that he's the obvious choice to fill that gap. He was the best regular third baseman the franchise has ever known.

The native Missourian was one of 14 children, three of whom (including Clete and Cloyd) played in the major leagues. A pitcher initially, his bat proved too lively to waste, and he became the third-base starter for St. Louis at age 23. Boyer reached the pinnacle of his career in 1964, when he made his 11th All-Star team, led the league with 119 RBI, won its MVP Award, and played brilliantly in the World Series conquest of the Yankees. Only Stan Musial and Albert Pujols have hit more home runs in a Cardinals uniform, and only Mike Schmidt and Scott Rolen have won more than his five National League Gold Gloves at third.

What truly distinguished Boyer, however, was his abiding class and serene leadership. Forever known as "The Captain" among those with whom he played, No. 14 was the ultimate teammate. Scores of Cardinals fans still venerate him as their favorite player.

Clete maintains to this day that, had his brother plied his trade under the floodlights of New York, Ken would have been immortalized in Cooperstown long ago.

Pure Gold in Center Field

When asked to nominate the best trade the Cardinals ever made, "Ernie Broglio for Lou Brock" is usually a fan's knee-jerk response. Fair enough, but "three pitchers, who ended up winning a total of six games in Cincinnati, for Curt Flood" would be a good answer as well.

Heisted from the Reds as a teen in the winter of 1957, Flood was a part-timer for two-and-a-half years under narrow-minded manager Solly Hemus, whom the center fielder remarked many years later, "didn't

As a center fielder, Curt Flood was a profile in baseball elegance.

FLOOD'S DEFIANCE

"I do not feel I am a piece of property to be bought and sold," wrote Curt Flood to Commissioner Bowie Kuhn when the Cardinals attempted to deal him to the Phillies. "Any system which produces that result violates my basic right as a citizen."

With those words, baseball's free agency movement was galvanized. Flood brought his suit all the way to the U.S. Supreme Court to assert his autonomy. He lost at every step and chose to sit out the 1970 season, but he succeeded in exposing the game's underbelly of injustice in matters of player control. Within seven years of Flood's daring defiance, free agency was established.

Elysian Fields
Quarterly
THE BASEBALL REVIEW

Baseball: Deregulation and Free Enterprise
by Eugene J. McCarthy
Vol. 12 / No. 1 • 1993

really care for me or Bob Gibson." But for Johnny Keane, Flood developed into a three-time All-Star, a co-captain of three pennant winners, and the successor to Willie Mays as baseball's finest defensive center fielder.

Curt's range, grace, and strong arm were a hallmark of the great Cardinals teams of the 1960s. He won a Gold Glove Award the last seven years of the decade, and for a time he held records for most consecutive games played and chances handled by an outfielder without an error.

Nor was he an easy out. Most often slotted first or second in the batting order, he whacked .293 in 15 seasons. After the 1969 season, Flood was traded and put up enough of a fuss about it that he changed the game.

For his stance against baseball's reserve clause, Flood has been compared to many people—from Jackie Robinson to Rosa Parks to Muhammad Ali. He challenged the game's economics, he said, because "I found that all of those rights that these great Americans were dying for [in Vietnam], I didn't have in my own profession."

Cardinals Soar in '64

Far right: The Cards needed seven games to beat the Yankees and win the 1964 World Series. Bob Gibson won two games, and Tim Mc-Carver led the offense with a .478 batting average.

Below: The 1964 Cardinals made up 12 games in the standings in the final 43 days of the season.

From 1947 to 1963, only five teams in the majors won more games than the Cards, yet they had no championships to show for it. For the last seven of those years, however, general manager Bing Devine was patiently assembling a durable winner. In addition to expanding the team's scouting horizons to include more players of color, his astute trades yielded half of 1964's starting lineup. Devine's pièce de résistance came on June 15 of that season. Having never found an acceptable heir to Stan Musial in left

field, he pulled off a brazen deal to land swift youngster Lou Brock from the Cubs.

"Presto," recalls pitcher Bob Gibson, "we were transformed."

With Brock hitting .348 and stealing 33 bases in his 103 games, the Cardinals—standing 28–31 at the time of the trade—took flight. Before long, the Cards—6½ games back on September 20—found themselves in a free-for-all five-team pennant race that wound all the way into October. On

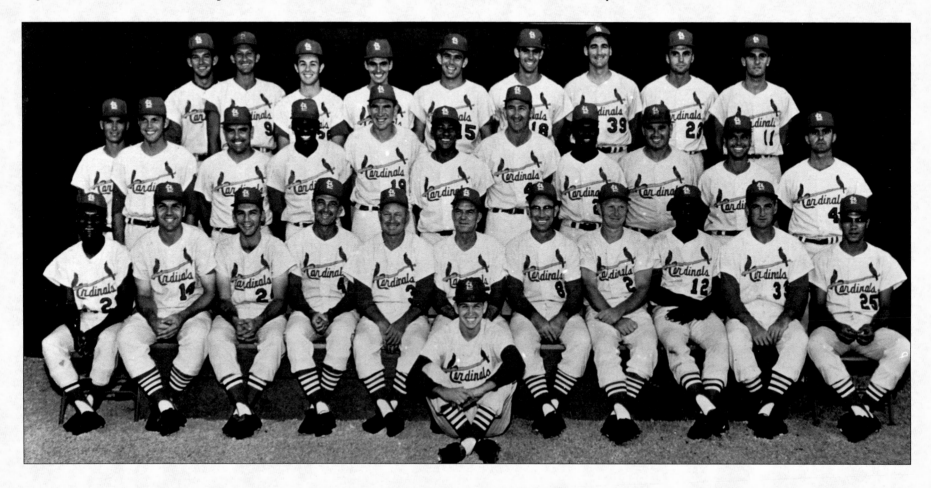

Ken Boyer (left), Tim McCarver (center), and Mike Shannon were asked to pose together after being the only three Cardinals to hit home runs in the first five games of the 1964 World Series. Boyer added another in the Game 7 win.

the final day, a St. Louis win coupled with a Cincinnati loss slithered Johnny Keane's squad to the top of the standings. Gussie Busch had his first pennant.

As usual, the Yankees were the AL champs and, as usual, they were the heavy World Series favorites. Although the Cards established credibility by hammering a sore-armed Whitey Ford in the opener, their own ace, Bob Gibson, fared no better in Game 2, losing 8–3. The teams' superstar sluggers settled the next two contests: Mickey Mantle with a game-ending home run, then Ken Boyer with a sixth-inning grand slam to slingshot the Cards from a 3–0 debit to a 4–3 win.

Game 5 was just as taut. Gibson was within an out of a shutout when he surrendered a tying two-run homer, but battery mate Tim

McCarver bailed him out with a three-run shot in the tenth. Back in St. Louis, the Yankees' home-run bats forced a Game 7 showdown. Gibby volunteered to start on two days' rest and, exhausted, nearly gave back a 6–0 lead before holding on to clinch, 7–5.

Despite all the winning, there were two important losses in the Cardinals' historic season. Busch, with special consultant Branch Rickey in his ear, had gone personnel shopping during the summer. Stunningly, he fired Bing Devine in August. A disgusted Keane, just as unexpectedly, resigned the day after the World Series win to become manager of the Yankees. His more-than-worthy successor in the Cardinals dugout was to be Red Schoendienst. As for "Der Bingle," the stamp of his sagacity would be felt long past 1964.

Liberated from his incarceration of reluctant celebrity in New York, Roger Maris became a cherished Redbird leader and 1967 World Series hero.

THE RADIO BROADCAST TEAM OF JACK BUCK AND HARRY CARAY IN THE 1950S AND 1960S WAS AMONG THE BEST IN MAJOR-LEAGUE BASEBALL, ESPECIALLY WHEN THE PENNANT WAS AT STAKE, AS WAS THE CASE IN 1964.

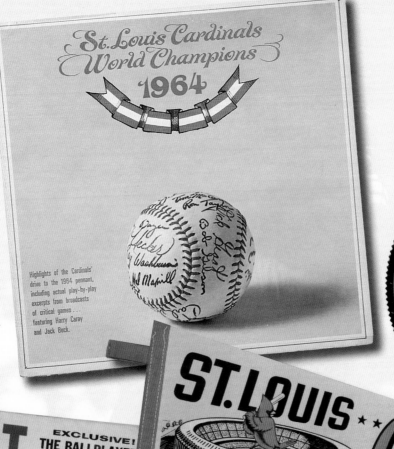

St. Louis Cardinals
World Champions
1964

Highlights of the Cardinals' drive to the 1964 pennant, including actual play-by-play excerpts from broadcasts of critical games . . . featuring Harry Caray and Jack Buck.

ONE REASON FOR THE CARDINALS' SUCCESS IN THE 1960S WAS A TRADE PULLED OFF BY GENERAL MANAGER BING DEVINE PRIOR TO THE 1958 SEASON, WHEN HE ACQUIRED A 20-YEAR-OLD OUTFIELDER NAMED CURT FLOOD FROM THE CINCINNATI REDS.

139 Cardinals   Curt Flood OF

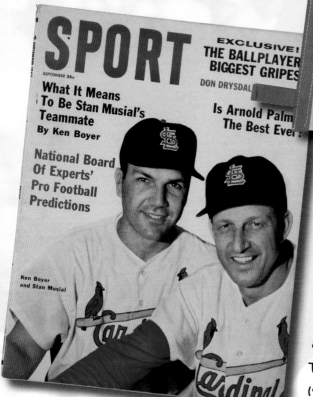

SPORT
SEPTEMBER 35¢
What It Means To Be Stan Musial's Teammate
By Ken Boyer

National Board Of Experts' Pro Football Predictions

EXCLUSIVE!
THE BALLPLAYERS' BIGGEST GRIPES
DON DRYSDALE

Is Arnold Palmer The Best Ever?

Ken Boyer and Stan Musial

ST. LOUIS ★★★
Cardinals ★

JUST AS STAN MUSIAL WAS ENTERING THE LATTER YEARS OF HIS LONG AND GLORIOUS CAREER IN ST. LOUIS, ANOTHER STAR EMERGED TO TAKE HIS PLACE AS THE LEADER OF THE CARDINALS: KEN BOYER. THE TWO PLAYED TOGETHER FROM 1955 UNTIL 1963.

IN ADDITION TO WINNING THREE PENNANTS AND TWO WORLD SERIES TITLES IN THE 1960S, THE CARDINALS MOVED INTO THE NEW BUSCH STADIUM IN DOWNTOWN ST. LOUIS IN 1966. THE STADIUM WOULD BE THE TEAM'S HOME FOR THE NEXT 40 SEASONS.

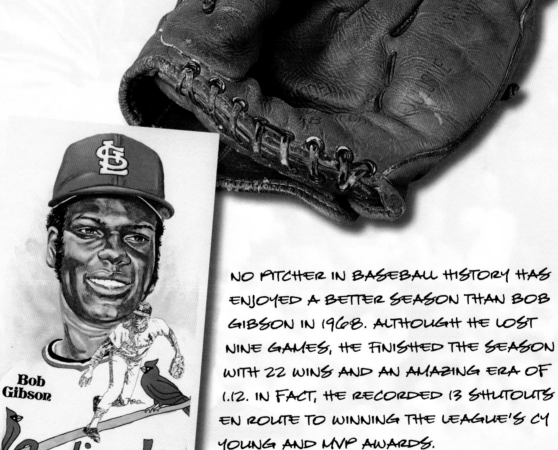

On Today's Editorial Page
Mr. McNamara and the World
Bank: Editorial
The Passenger Train Losses:
Editorial

ST. LOUIS POST-DISPATCH

FINAL
★ ★ ★
Closing Stock Market Prices
Pages 5D and 6D

72 PAGES

Price 10c Home Delivery $3.00 a Month

VOL. 90 NO. 273

© 1968, St. Louis Post-Dispatch

THURSDAY, OCTOBER 3, 1968

Cardinal pitcher Bob Gibson firing the ball to a Detroit batter in the first inning of the opening World Series game yesterday. The Redbird ace struck out a record 17 batters in posting a 4-0 victory. It was also his sixth consecutive complete-game World Series victory, another record. (Post-Dispatch Photograph by Gene Pospeshil)

Tigers Score Early With Home Runs In Second Game of the World Series

By Bob Broeg
Post-Dispatch Sports Editor

Detroit's advertised power displayed itself today in the second game of the 1968 World Series at Busch Memorial Stadium. As a result, the Cardinals' starting pitcher, failed to survive the sixth inning.

After seven innings, Detroit led. And led.

Another crowd of 54,692 watched the Tigers go to the long ball early as they routed Briles.

Slugger Willie Horton, who hit 36 homers in the American League season, homered in the second inning. The Detroit pitcher, Mickey Lolich, who had not hit a home run in six major league seasons, reached the fence in the third, and Norm Cash, who belted 25 in the regular season, hit a home run in the sixth.

The Cardinals finally broke through in the sixth inning, scoring one run when Brock walked, stole second, and moved around on an infield hit by Flood and a looping hit by Cepeda.

The second game was played in weather remarkably different from yesterday's opener. The game-time temperature, 69, was 20 degrees lower, as reflected by spectators wearing coats, jackets and more colorful attire. The skies had cleared by the time the umpires came out to accept the lineup cards, which showed just one change, other than a rare pitchers.

For the Cardinals, a lefthanded starter, Ron Davis played right field, rather than Roger Maris. Davis batted seventh behind Lou Brock, left field; Julian Javier, second base; Curt Flood, center field; Orlando Cepeda, first base; Mike Shannon, third base, and Tim McCarver, catcher.

The shortstop, Dal Maxvill, and starting pitcher, Nelson Briles, brought up the bottom of the batting order.

Detroit Lineup

Detroit's lineup was the same

Kaline, right field; Norm Cash, first base; Willie Horton, left field; Jim Northrup, center field; Bill Freehan, catcher; Don Wert, third base, and Lolich.

The 27-year-old Lolich, making his first Series appearance, owned a 17-9 regular-season record in the American League. Briles, 25, author of a 5-2 third-game victory over the Boston Red Sox in last year's World Series, had a 19-11 record this season in National League competition.

First Batter

Opening today's second game, Briles was hot with his first two pitches to McAuliffe. The Detroit second baseman then hit the next pitch smartly on the ground, but directly to Cepeda, who waved Briles away and made the putout unassisted.

Stanley hit Briles's third delivery for an opposite-field fly to Davis in medium right field. And the St. Louis pitcher was applauded for a 1-2-1 inning

throw out the first ball. This time, though no one threw out Maxvill.

Medwick as the late commissioner, Judge K. M. Landis, did when Detroit threw debris at the Redbird left fielder after a baseline altercation.

Lolich began impressively, too. The Cardinals' leadoff man, Brock, went out on three pitches as the Detroit lefthander caught the outside corner with a curve for a called third strike.

Now, however, Mickey had to face Redbird righthanded hitters, and he encountered trouble that brought a cheer of encouragement to the Cardinals. Lolich's first pitch to Javier was wild. Hoolie hammered the next one for a high-hopping single over Wert's head into left field. And Flood walked on just four pitches.

At this point, the Detroit defense came to Lolich's aid, to

TURN TO PAGE 16, COLUMN 1

Senator Eugene J. McCarthy was a cool, dispassionate, Series observer from his seat behind home plate. McCarthy, a long-time baseball player, is interpreting the Series.

A passionate American League fan, David Eisenhower, rooted for the Tigers. Julie Nixon, his fiance, took a bipartisan interest in the Cardinals. (Post-Dispatch Photo.

Bob Gibson

THE REDBIRDS WERE GETTING USED TO PLAYING IN THE WORLD SERIES BY 1968, BUT THEY WERE STILL FRONT PAGE NEWS IN ST. LOUIS.

IN 1958, KEN BOYER BECAME THE FIRST CARDINAL TO EVER WIN A GOLD GLOVE, THE FIRST OF FIVE HE WOULD WIN IN HIS 11-YEAR CAREER IN ST. LOUIS. HE EVENTUALLY WAS TRADED TO THE METS AFTER THE 1965 SEASON, BUT LATER HE RETURNED TO ST. LOUIS TO SERVE A STINT AS THE TEAM'S MANAGER.

NO PITCHER IN BASEBALL HISTORY HAS ENJOYED A BETTER SEASON THAN BOB GIBSON IN 1968. ALTHOUGH HE LOST NINE GAMES, HE FINISHED THE SEASON WITH 22 WINS AND AN AMAZING ERA OF 1.12. IN FACT, HE RECORDED 13 SHUTOUTS EN ROUTE TO WINNING THE LEAGUE'S CY YOUNG AND MVP AWARDS.

Bob Gibson was one of the greatest all-around athletes to play the game. There have been few pitchers to hit or field his position as deftly. While playing for the Harlem Globetrotters, he was renown for his reverse dunks.

Bullet Bob

Everything about Bob Gibson, save his ERA, was outsized—his fastball, his confidence, his detachment, his compassion, his humor, his humor*lessness*, his intelligence, and, especially, his heart. One of the greatest athletes ever to play *any* sport, he transcended even those special gifts with a courage and tenacity that made him one of the best pitchers ever and, for one year, perhaps the best there ever was.

A product of such disadvantage as a child that he was beset at various times by rickets, rat-bite fever, life-threatening asthma, and a heart murmur, Gibson became better known as a basketball player—the first African-American to play at Creighton and then as a Harlem Globetrotter who proved too competitive for all the horseplay. He signed with the Cardinals in 1957, and two years later he gave up a home run to the first major-leaguer he faced. He suffered few other humbling moments.

"Bullet Bob" spent 17 seasons with St. Louis, during which he set franchise records for wins (251) and strikeouts (3,117). He won the 1968 NL MVP and Cy Young Awards, two World Series MVP Awards, and another Cy in 1970. By hitting 24 home runs and capturing nine consecutive Gold Gloves, he made himself even tougher to beat.

In 1967, Gibby's leg was broken by a line drive off the bat of Roberto Clemente. He threw several more pitches before missing almost two months, then returned in time to give perhaps the greatest composite World Series pitching performance ever. Each of his three starts against the Red Sox were complete-game victories (including Game 7), during which he allowed a mere three runs total. Yet what that foreshadowed was nothing less than epic.

"Hoot" had a 1968 ERA of 1.12—still the game's lowest since 1914—and this was the summation of a season of matchless stats. He fired 13 shutouts, won 22 times despite losing two 1–0 games, averaged 8.97 innings per start, was not once removed in the middle of an inning, led the league with 268 strikeouts, allowed only two earned runs in a 95-inning stretch, compiled a 0.57 ERA in his wins and a 2.14 mark in his *losses*, held batters to only ten hits in 93 at-bats with runners in scoring position and two outs, and retired 888 of the 1,161 batters he faced. His magnum opus was a record 17-strikeout shutout of the Tigers in the World Series opener.

Only marginally more hittable the next year, Gibson's fourth of five 20-win seasons was accented by the same number of complete games as in 1968 and one more strikeout, plus a 2.18 ERA. Of those two memorable campaigns, his catcher Tim McCarver has written, "Gibby was an awesome, over-powering, dominant pitcher ... there was nothing he couldn't do."

Bob Gibson's number 45 is one of nine uniform numbers the Cardinals have retired in honor of a great player. The only other prominent player in team history who wore 45 was pitcher Von McDaniel in 1957 and 1958.

All-Star Reds outfielder Vada Pinson regarded Gibson as "the meanest man alive" (until they were teammates). Manager Johnny Keane preferred to dispatch his pitching coach to remove Gibby from a game, thus dodging the inevitable vile epithet. Most of the sports media were too intimidated even to approach him. Opposing batters wilted before his scornful scowl and red-hot high-rider. Fans came in droves to see him pitch but usually found him unapproachable. And with that image, Gibson was content. It was more than an image; it was a mystique.

Gibby's ERA was 1.67 in the 1968 World Series, but the rest of the staff's was 6.94, and even Gibson faltered in Game 7 as the Redbirds bowed to the Tigers.

Redbirds Outlast the Red Sox

The sheen of the 1964 World Series triumph dulled quickly. Not only did the winning fade away over the next two seasons, an era did as well. Bygone heroes such as first baseman Bill White, shortstop Dick Groat, and third baseman Ken Boyer were traded. And, in May of 1966, old Sportsman's Park was abandoned for sparkling new Busch Memorial Stadium on the riverfront.

Come 1967, though, something was different, both material and subtle. Afield, there were three key new faces: an old veteran to professionalize the lineup (Roger Maris), a bespectacled middle-aged rookie who would lead the staff in wins (Dick Hughes), and a 22-year-old taking his first steps toward Cooperstown (lefty Steve Carlton). But there also was a more buoyant vibe. Spiritual compass Orlando Cepeda hung a catchy nickname, *El Birdos*, on his mates. A "lucky" red and white ball became part of the infield practice ritual. The personalities homogenized, spending long hours talking baseball together in the clubhouse after games. "I've never seen a team like that," said Cepeda. "We were a team. No superstars."

Were Bob Gibson a mere mortal in the 1967 fall classic, Roger Maris might have been its MVP. This was a rare swing-and-a-miss, as he pelted Red Sox pitchers for ten hits and a Series-high seven RBI.

Top left: Nellie Briles was an overlooked star in 1967. After Gibson broke his leg, Briles stepped into the rotation and won nine consecutive decisions with a 1.49 ERA.

Bottom right: Not only is Lou Brock tied with Eddie Collins for most stolen bases (14) in World Series history, he also ranks among the top ten in Series batting average (.391), slugging percentage (.655), and extra-base hits (13).

THE CHA CHA IN ST. LOUIS

Most Cardinals fans wouldn't have agreed at the time, but their club's trade of Ray Sadecki for Orlando Cepeda in 1966 was a coup. Sadecki fizzled in San Francisco, but "Cha Cha" sizzled in St. Louis. In 1967, Cepeda made his 11th All-Star team, led the National League with 111 RBI, swatted .325, powered 25 homers, and became the circuit's first unanimous MVP since 1936. "The Baby Bull" was gone after a subpar 1968 season, but for one year his loud lumber, earsplitting salsa music, and high-frequency energy sparked a champion.

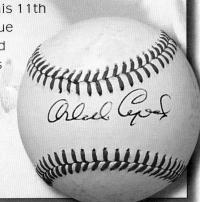

The 1967 Cardinals clearly were more than the sum of their parts. Even with extended injury absences by Bob Gibson and Curt Flood, they coasted to 101 wins and the pennant. Next up: the long-suffering Boston Red Sox, chasing their "Impossible Dream" in what would become an archetypal World Series.

Gibby got the opening call, of course, and delivered a 2–1 victory. Then Julian Javier saved the Cards from the ignominy of being the second team to be no-hit in a Series game with an eighth-inning double off Jim Lonborg as the Red Sox eased to a win.

St. Louis's pitching turned dominant the next two meetings. Young Nellie Briles stymied the Red Sox, 5–2, and Gibson went one better with a five-hit shutout. But Boston scuffled back on a three-hitter by Lonborg

and a Game 6 long-ball assault to force a rubber match. This time it was Gibby's turn to spin a three-hitter. He even blasted a home run himself in a 7–2 triumph. "Bullet Bob" was the obvious MVP, but it was Lou Brock's Series-record seven steals and Maris's seven RBI that fueled the offense.

Gussie Busch felt this was merely an early salvo in a new Cardinals dynasty.

Above: It was the acquisition of first baseman Orlando Cepeda from the Giants during the 1966 season that helped make the Cardinals a pennant-winning team in 1967 and 1968. Cepeda was named the league's MVP in 1967.

The Heartbreak of '68

For 162 games, the 1968 season seemed like an instant replay of 1967. The top nine hitters and four-fifths of the starting rotation were precisely the same as the year before. So was the ease with which the Cardinals humbled the National League. If anything had changed, it was perhaps that some of the team's unpretentious accord had evolved into flashy swagger. This was, after all, what a *Sports Illustrated* cover revealed to be the "Highest Paid Team in Baseball History." The payroll for the Redbirds' nine starters and manager was $607,000.

Twice in the first four games of the 1968 fall classic against the Detroit Tigers, Bob Gibson made history. His shutout with an unprecedented 17 strikeouts in the opener rivals Don Larsen's perfect game as the greatest-ever World Series pitching performance. Game 4 was Gibby's seventh consecutive Series win (still a record), giving the Cards a seemingly insurmountable three-to-one advantage.

Even after the Tigers took the next two games, prospects were bright with Gibson toeing the rubber for the deciding game at Busch. Matching zeroes with Mickey Lolich, he retired 20 of the first 21 batters before

Cardinal fans who purchased World Series tickets for the 1968 games against Detroit thought they would be celebrating a second consecutive championship, but the Tigers had other ideas, beating the Cardinals in seven games.

An Orlando Cepeda three-run homer sewed up a Game 3 victory in the 1968 World Series. It was the last dance for "Cha Cha," however, as Gussie Busch dismantled a team he considered overpaid and under-achieving after losing the Series to the Tigers in seven games.

Detroit strung together four straight hits to win a 4–1 stunner. It was the first time the Cardinals had ever lost a Game 7. They would wait 14 years for another one—a very long time to cope with the collapse of 1968.

Electrifying Lou

Brock tore up the basepaths for seven stolen bases in the 1968 World Series, tying his own record set the year before. More than just his wheels went into it. He used to film pitchers' motions from the dugout with an 8mm movie camera.

A 10-year-old Lou Brock knew zilch about Stan Musial when he was assigned to deliver an oral report to his class about great ballplayers as a punishment for flicking a spitball. In 1964, when Brock's electrifying speed and rally-rousing bat conjured a world championship, "The Man" himself appraised, "The Cardinals wouldn't have won with *me* in left field."

That season commenced a thrill-a-minute, 16-year ride with Brock in left for St. Louis. Playing past his 40th birthday, he set the game's all-time stolen base records (since broken by Rickey Henderson) of 118 in a season and 938 in a career. He also stung 3,023 hits, batted .300 for a season eight times, and made six All-Star teams. Lou's rpms revved even higher in the World Series. In 21 games, he hit .391 with 13 extra-base hits while thieving 14 bags in his last 14 contests.

Brock is the only man to have swept the Lou Gehrig, Hutch, Roberto Clemente, and Bobby Bragan Youth Foundation Lifetime Achievement awards, all presented for character and off-field contributions. While he was still active in 1978, one was named after him: the Lou Brock Award, which goes to the National League stolen base champ.

When Brock slid safely into this base on August 29, 1977, he eclipsed Ty Cobb's record of 893 steals. The very next day was the 72nd anniversary of Cobb's major-league debut.

WHAT A STEAL!

The team's 1964 trade of pitcher Ernie Broglio to the Cubs for Brock was wildly popular in Chicago. "Thank you, thank you, you lovely St. Louis Cardinals," wrote Bob Smith of the *Chicago Daily News*. "Nice doing business with you. Please call again anytime." Even Cardinals players furtively shared his sentiment. Broglio, who'd won 60 games the previous four years, was well liked; Brock was considered a baseball tenderfoot who didn't know a fungo bat from a broomstick. Almost instantly the clubhouse perception of the swap was altered, as the kid won over his teammates with his respect, coachability, and astounding talent. Meanwhile, Broglio won only seven more games.

WORLD SERIES NEXT! GO! GO! GO!

CHAMPION

St. Louis Cardinals

A SPECIAL SECTION
IN HONOR OF THE 1967
NATIONAL LEAGUE CHAMPION
ST. LOUIS BASEBALL CARDINALS

Stan Musial, General Manager

Red Schoendienst, Field Manager

ST. LOUIS POST-DISPATCH   SUNDAY, OCTOBER 1, 1967

1968
WORLD SERIES
ST. LOUIS CARDINALS VS. DETROIT TIGERS

BUSCH MEMORIAL STADIUM
OFFICIAL PROGRAM $1.00

THE FIRST TIME THE WORLD SERIES WAS PLAYED IN THE NEW BUSCH STADIUM WAS 1967, AND THE NATIONAL LEAGUE CHAMPS WERE EXCITED TO MEET THE BOSTON RED SOX THERE.

BEFORE 1968, THE CARDINALS AND TIGERS HAD MET IN THE WORLD SERIES JUST ONCE BEFORE, IN 1934. THE TIGERS AVENGED THEIR 1934 LOSS BY COMING BACK IN THE 1968 SERIES FROM A 3-1 DEFICIT TO WIN THE FINAL THREE GAMES AND CLAIM THE TITLE OF WORLD SERIES CHAMPION.

CARDINAL FANS WERE EAGER TO SUPPORT THEIR TEAM IN THE 1967 WORLD SERIES AND QUICKLY PURCHASED ALL AVAILABLE TICKETS.

WHEN THE CARDINALS ACQUIRED LOU BROCK, SHOWN RUNNING ON THIS POSTCARD, FROM THE CUBS IN A 1964 SIX-PLAYER DEAL, MANY ST. LOUIS FANS THOUGHT THE TEAM HAD MADE A TERRIBLE DECISION IN SENDING PITCHER ERNIE BROGLIO TO CHICAGO.

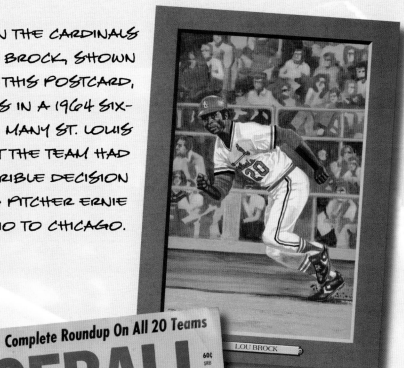

LOU BROCK

RED SCHOENDIENST APPEARS ON THIS PEREZ-STEELE POSTCARD. A FORMER CARDINAL PLAYER, HE TOOK OVER AS THE TEAM'S MANAGER WHEN JOHNNY KEANE QUIT AFTER THE 1964 WORLD SERIES. SCHOENDIENST GUIDED THE CARDINALS FOR THE NEXT 12 YEARS, BECOMING THE FRANCHISE'S WINNINGEST MANAGER UNTIL TONY LA RUSSA PASSED HIS CAREER TOTAL OF 1,041 WINS.

Red Schoendienst

PEREZ

Cardinals

THE STARS OF THE 1967 WORLD SERIES FOR THE CARDINALS WERE LOU BROCK AND BOB GIBSON, GIVING THEM PLENTY OF NATIONAL PUBLICITY IN 1968 AS THEY WERE FEATURED IN SUCH SPORTS MAGAZINES AS THIS ISSUE OF *BASEBALL*. BROCK HIT .414 AND STOLE A RECORD SEVEN BASES AGAINST THE RED SOX, WHILE GIBSON NOTCHED THREE OF THE FOUR ST. LOUIS WINS, ALL COMPLETE-GAME EFFORTS.

Moonman Shannon

Mike Shannon's hometown-boy-makes-good tale might best be expressed in his own fractured metaphor, uttered during one of his more than 5,000 Cardinal radio broadcasts: "Well, folks, this game began as a tiny worm and is blossoming into a large cobra."

Born in St. Louis, Shannon essentially never left. The Cards signed him out of the University of Missouri, and he played for no one else in his 13-year pro career. Shannon's steady dependability on the field was punctuated with moments of eye-opening virtuosity. "Moonman" was the only player to drive in at least 75 runs for both 1967 and 1968 pennant-winners, and he hit one memorable home run in each of his three World Series. An outfielder by trade, he gladly converted to third base to accommodate Roger Maris in 1967.

His attitude was a key to the championship chemistry.

After a kidney disease ended his playing career at age 31, Shannon entered the front office and then, in 1972, the radio booth. After many years as "co-pilot" on KMOX, Shannon became the team's lead voice upon Jack Buck's death in 2002. His shameless beer promos, homespun (occasionally unintentional) humor, and predictable catchphrases ("Get up, baby, get up" on promising fly balls) have been comforting constants to listeners for more than three decades.

In 1966, the same year that Shannon first became an everyday player, the Gateway Arch was dedicated. Today, the two hold comparable stature as St. Louis institutions.

The 2007 season marked a half-century in the Cardinals organization for Mike Shannon as a player, front office exec, and broadcaster. He is shown here batting in the 1964 World Series in which he hit a key opening-game home run off the Yankees' Whitey Ford.

A Rock Behind the Plate

Tim McCarver will forever be pegged in St. Louis as "Bob Gibson's catcher." In his view, that's probably the highest compliment he could be paid. McCarver was one of the few who could coexist with the temperamental ace—and he almost certainly made him a better pitcher.

Timmy, however, enjoyed a few front-and-center moments of his own. In 1959, at age 17, he was the youngest Cardinal in 52 years. In the 1964 World Series, he hit .478, winning Game 5 with a tenth-inning homer. In 1966, he became the first catcher since 1884 to lead a league in triples. Despite his customarily humble offensive stats, the Cards' comical, cocky co-captain was runner-up to Orlando Cepeda as the 1967 NL MVP. He caught at least one game in 20 seasons (only seven players have done so in more), and he was the rare player to see action in four separate decades.

McCarver, however, drew much closer to the pinnacle of his profession after he traded his mask for a mic. For more than a quarter-century, the multiple Emmy winner has been an acclaimed, sometimes polarizing, baseball TV and radio analyst for several major networks and teams.

Tim McCarver was the Cards' regular catcher during the glory days of the 1960s, and he once said how "lucky" he was to be Bob Gibson's battery mate. "Every time he pitches," he said, "the other team doesn't score."

DEVINE INFLUENCE

It spoke in equal voice to the capriciousness of the Cardinals' head office and his own expertise that Bing Devine was named 1964 Executive of the Year two months after the Cardinals sacked him and four years before he became the first general manager rehired by the same team that fired him. The former Cards office boy rose through the ranks to craft three Redbird pennant-winners—not to mention the 1969 "Miracle Mets" between his stints in St. Louis. Devine died at age 90 in 2007, "still working for the Cardinals," according to his wife, Mary. "I tell you he would have worked for them for free."

Top left: It was Yankees Hall of Fame catcher Bill Dickey, then a Cardinals scout, who first spotted a 15-year-old Tim McCarver. Two years later, McCarver was in The Show. His cerebral approach to the game has defined his long career as a player, broadcaster, and author.

Immediate left: McCarver managed only as many hits (three) as Bob Gibson had complete game victories in the 1967 Series, but his savvy game-calling and fearless leadership were, as always, vital to the success of "Hoot" and the rest of the Cardinals.

Red's Steady Hand

Red Schoendienst was a self-made player, but he was born to be a manager. Drawing from a 19-year playing career and his detailed understanding of the game's nuances, he applied his wisdom in a calm but firm, decisive but evenhanded manner that made his players revere him.

Initially, Schoendienst relished the teaching and coaching aspects of the job far more, but he grew into an adroit handler of men. In the spring of 1968, he laid down but two rules for them: "Run everything out and be in by 12." Mistakes were corrected in private, not before the eyes of teammates or the ears of the media. That sort of trust and respect, he reasoned, would inspire loyalty in return. "You

After Johnny Keane (right) abruptly resigned following the 1964 World Series win, the rumor was that he'd be succeeded by Leo Durocher. Instead, the managerial reins were turned over—fortuitously, as it turned out—to popular Cardinals Hall of Famer Red Schoendienst (left).

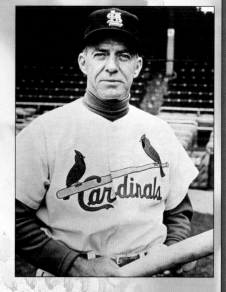

KEANE SKIPS TOWN

The day after his team's 1964 World Series win, Gussie Busch called a press conference to announce the rehiring of Johnny Keane as manager. Fifteen minutes after its scheduled start, Keane handed the owner his letter of resignation.

For 27 years, Johnny had been a loyal Cardinal in one capacity or another, but upon learning that summer that Busch had been rummaging around for his potential replacement, he tired of the one-way street. The team's great finish had prompted Busch to reconsider, but it was too late: His skipper had secretly signed a contract to manage the 1965 Yankees *before* the 1964 World Series started. In less than two years in New York, Keane was fired. In less than three, he had passed away.

have to know what kind of players you have, and how to talk to them," he said. "I got to know each individual. I tried to be fair and tried not to show the players up."

Under his direction from 1965 to 1976, the Cardinals showed up plenty of opponents. Red helmed a World Series champ in his third year and a pennant winner in his fourth. Succeeding teams performed under a relative talent deficit, but he pinched out three second-place divisional finishes. Until Tony La Russa overtook him in 2007, he was the franchise's managerial wins leader with 1,041.

From Slugger to President

One of the keys to the Cardinals' success in 1964 was first baseman Bill White, acquired from the San Francisco Giants in a four-player trade in 1959. The 25-year-old White and third baseman Ray Jablonski were sent to the Cards for two players.

Returning to the San Francisco Giants from military service in 1958, a 24-year-old Bill White could not beat out rookie Orlando Cepeda for the first base job. Eight years later, Cepeda replaced White in St. Louis. In between, Bill amassed more extra-base knocks and hit for a higher batting average than any other Cardinal.

The popular left-handed hitter was one of those players who was easily taken for granted. White never led the league in anything sexier than plate appearances. He annually hovered around 20 homers, a .300 average, and 100 RBI, however, and his seven consecutive Gold Gloves were a National League first base record until another Cardinal, Keith Hernandez, monopolized the award in the 1980s. "I wasn't a great athlete," he said. "I just worked harder than anybody else."

White's legacy with the Cardinals, and indeed with the game itself, outreached the back of his baseball card. An extraordinarily strong and intelligent man who nearly made a career of medicine, he was one of the more vocal critics of the racist elements—experienced firsthand in minor-league assignments and during spring trainings in the South—that still blemished baseball in the 1950s and 1960s. In 1961, he was instrumental in convincing the Cards to

Bill White was a pillar of strength in the lineup, in the clubhouse, and as a voice of equality for African-Americans in baseball. The future National League president was an All-Star in five seasons and a .300 hitter with at least 20 homers and 100 ribbies in three straight years.

abandon their long-established segregated springtime hotels in St. Petersburg, Florida.

Even before he was traded to Philadelphia, White hosted (on a dare from Harry Caray) a five-minute radio show on KMOX. Later he was the first African-American TV play-by-play man for a big-league team, the Yankees. In 1989, he took a large pay cut to accept the presidency of the National League, then the most powerful position ever afforded a black man in a major sport. Bill abruptly resigned in 1994 to go fishing, leaving the sport to lament the big one that got away.

Former Cards Manager Dyer Succumbs at 63

april 20, 1964

HOUSTON (AP)—Eddie Dyer, manager of the 1946 world champion St. Louis Cardinals, died Monday at the age of 63. He had suffered a stroke Jan. 2, 1963.

After 23 years as a player, manager, and coach, Dyer returned to Houston in 1948 and was quite successful with business interests that included insurance, oil, and real estate. Howie Pollet and Jeff Cross, two former Cardinal stars, were business associates.

Dyer's Cardinals won the world championship by defeating the Boston Red Sox the first year he was a major league manager. He quit baseball after the 1948 season when Fred Saigh, then the Cardinal owner, offered him only a one-year contract.

A left-handed pitcher, Dyer jumped from the Rice University campus to the Cardinals in 1925 and blanked the Chicago Cubs, 3-0, in his first major league starting assignment.

He remained with the Cardinal organization throughout his professional career becoming a manager after developing a sore arm.

He managed Texas league championship teams in Houston in 1939, 1940, and 1941 and was named minor league Manager of the Year in 1942 for his work at Columbus, Ohio.

Dyer was born Oct. 11, 1900, at Morgan City, La., where he was captain of his high school football team. At Rice, he played football and baseball.

He was in the Rice class of 1924 but did not graduate until 1936, when he returned to the campus as a freshman football coach and completed a few hours work needed for his degree.

Survivors include the widow, the former Geraldine Jennings a Rice sweetheart in 1925, and a son, Eddie Jr., a business associate.

Funeral arrangements are pending.

Burns Park Winner

A LIFETIME CARDINAL, EDDIE DYER WAS BEST REMEMBERED AS THE MANAGER OF THE 1946 WORLD CHAMPIONS. THIS 1964 ARTICLE REPORTS ON HIS UNTIMELY DEATH.

FOR THE 30TH ANNIVERSARY OF BUSCH STADIUM IN 1996, THE CARDINALS ISSUED A SPECIAL COMMEMORATIVE PIN, WHICH INCLUDED THE OUTLINE OF THE STADIUM. THE BALLPARK'S DESIGN DIFFERS FROM THE OTHER "COOKIE-CUTTER" BALLPARKS OF ITS GENERATION BECAUSE OF THE ARCHES AROUND THE TOP OF THE STADIUM, BUILT TO SYMBOLIZE THE GATEWAY ARCH.

MANY FANS TOOK THE OPPORTUNITY TO PURCHASE SEATS FROM SPORTS-MAN'S PARK WHEN IT WAS TORN DOWN, AND NOW THEY HAVE THEM IN THEIR BASEMENTS, FAMILY ROOMS, OR OTHER ROOMS IN THEIR HOMES.

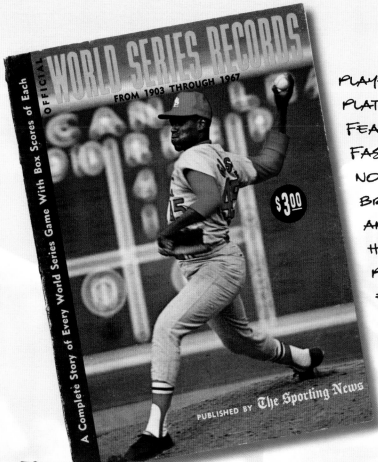

PLAYERS AT THE PLATE UNIVERSALLY FEARED A GIBSON FASTBALL. HE WAS NOT SHY ABOUT BRUSHING BACK ANY HITTER WHO HUGGED THE PLATE. HIS EXPLOITS ARE LISTED HERE IN WORLD SERIES RECORDS.

THE 1966 ALL-STAR GAME, SHOWN ON THIS POSTCARD, WAS PLAYED AT BUSCH STADIUM ON JULY 12. MAURY WILLS'S SINGLE DROVE IN TIM MCCARVER IN THE TENTH INNING TO GIVE THE NATIONAL LEAGUE A 2-1 VICTORY.

THE CARDINALS OF 1963 MARKED THE END OF AN ERA WITH STAN MUSIAL'S RETIREMENT AFTER 22 SEASONS OF WEARING THE UNIFORM WITH THE "BIRDS ON THE BAT." AT THE TIME OF HIS RETIREMENT, HE HELD THE MAJOR-LEAGUE RECORD FOR MOST EXTRA-BASE HITS AND THE MOST TOTAL BASES.

CHAPTER FIVE

THOSE '70S TEAMS
1970–1979

CARDINALS FANS WOULD just as soon forget the 1970s. There were no championships; the team played below .500; and a series of ruinous trades undid the winning continuity of the 1960s and imperiled the 1980s. Fortunately, there were several unforgettable performers and performances to tide over the faithful as Lou Brock shredded the stolen base record book and Bob Gibson became the National League's first 3,000-strikeout pitcher.

The Cardinals are distinguished by their glorious history. In 1976, this franchise celebrated the 100th anniversary of professional baseball in St. Louis.

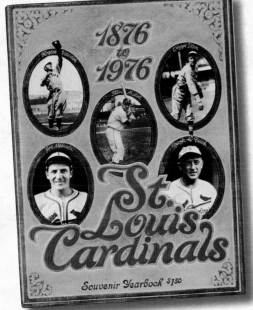

Bob Gibson walks off the mound after earning another line in the record book when he made the Reds' Cesar Geronimo his 3,000th career strikeout victim.

The 1967 World Series gave Lou Brock a chance to shine on the national stage, setting a record with seven stolen bases.

Joe's Torrid Bat

"Part of me has always been a Cardinal," Joe Torre said. The club got the best part of his distinguished playing career: six seasons during which he hit .308, averaged 93 RBI, and won the 1971 NL MVP Award and batting title.

Incongruously, considering his success as the former Yankees skipper, Joe Torre holds the record for most games played and managed (4,272) before reaching a World Series. The 1969–1974 Cardinals contributed 918 of those, but Torre was a beacon on those also-rans, leading the club in all the Triple Crown stats during his tenure.

Acquired from the Braves in 1969 in an unpopular trade for the popular Orlando Cepeda, Torre was the team's primary first baseman for three years, catcher for one, and third baseman for two. His run-producing bat was a constant.

In 1971, he put up a set of statistics not seen in St. Louis since another Joe (Medwick) did it 34 years earlier: a .363 batting average, a majors-leading 137 RBI, and 24 home runs. Torre was not only the runaway National League MVP, but he was also an unwitting billboard for the trendy Stillman water diet on which he'd lost 25 pounds over the winter to prepare for his switch to third.

On the field and in the clubhouse, Joe almost single-handedly made the Cardinals a 90-game winner that season. His teammates even called him "Assistant Coach," foreshadowing his enormously successful second career in which he became manager of all three franchises for which he'd played.

HITTING FOR THE CYCLE

Torre's last great individual feat for the Cardinals occurred on June 27, 1973, when he became the team's 11th player to hit for the cycle. In a 15–4 thrashing of the Pirates at Three Rivers Stadium, he ripped four different pitchers for hits, securing the "easy" part with a single in the ninth inning. Ironically, in his other at-bat, he bounced into one of his 284 double plays—the second most in NL history behind Hank Aaron.

96

A Stud at First Base

Whoever said first base was the place where sluggers went to die never saw Keith Hernandez play it. Revolutionizing the responsibilities and execution of the position, he could be found fielding a bunt down the third base line, counseling his pitchers, directing infield traffic, or positioning himself as a cutoff man. Many say there has been no one better.

The 783rd player drafted in 1971, Keith was a Cards regular five years later at age 22. Though he never hit 20 homers, he always had a nose for the moment, regularly driving in 80 to 100 runs. In 1979, he peaked with a league-leading .344 average and 105 RBI, tying for the NL MVP Award.

While defense is often impervious to measurement, statistics cannot evade Hernandez's brilliance. His 11 Gold Gloves are a first-base record, as were his 1,682 assists at the time of his retirement. Only one NLer at the position has ever turned more double plays, and Keith's .994 fielding percentage is one of the league's ten best.

In June 1983, at the peak of his career, Hernandez was traded for two journeyman pitchers. Manager Whitey Herzog wanted him gone. Keith could be a loudmouth and a clubhouse lawyer.

Keith reached legendary status in New York sports lore as a clutch component of the Mets' 1986 title—and with an appearance as himself on a classic episode of *Seinfeld* in which he allegedly spit on Kramer for calling him "a pretty boy." Not that he wasn't.

For nearly a decade (until the brass wearied of his audacity and bad habits), the Cardinals had perhaps the most complete active first baseman in base-ball: Keith Hernandez. In return for trading him to the Mets, they received two pitchers (Neil Allen and Rick Ownbey) who went 21–22 for them.

A Pair of Near Misses

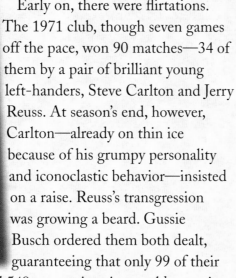

Following the 1968 pennant effort, the once-thriving Cardinals farm system began to parch; the economics of the game started leveling the playing field; players' behavior seemed to reflect the rebelliousness of the era; and two disastrous trades at the behest of their fuddy-duddy owner ensured the team would negotiate the decade without a title.

Early on, there were flirtations. The 1971 club, though seven games off the pace, won 90 matches—34 of them by a pair of brilliant young left-handers, Steve Carlton and Jerry Reuss. At season's end, however, Carlton—already on thin ice because of his grumpy personality and iconoclastic behavior—insisted on a raise. Reuss's transgression was growing a beard. Gussie Busch ordered them both dealt, guaranteeing that only 99 of their eventual 549 career victories would come in a Cardinals uniform.

The schizophrenic 1973 club was nothing special, but it played in a division full of nothing specials. The Cards started the year 5–20, then surged to a five-game NL East lead in early August. Then came another swoon before wins in their final five contests (highlighted by three consecutive shutouts) kept them mathematically viable—amazingly, at 81–81. They could do nothing but sit and

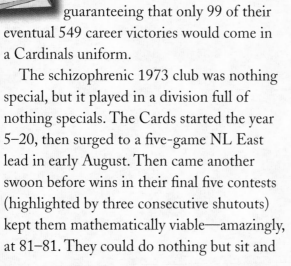

In the 1970s, the Cardinals did not enjoy much cumulative success as a team, but they certainly had no shortage of individual stars to cheer for, including Joe Torre, Bob Gibson, Ted Simmons, and Lou Brock, who appear on this Cardinals media guide.

agonize as the Mets defeated the Cubs in a makeup game to finish 82–79.

In 1974, with Lou Brock running wild to a record 118 stolen bases, Cardinals karma seemed reincarnate when the team won a 25-inning marathon on September 11 and a 17-inning game two nights later. Within four days, they led the division by 2½ games. On October 2, the season's final day, they needed a win in Montreal and a Pirates loss to the Cubs to tie Pittsburgh for the division title.

During Torre's tenure in St. Louis from 1969 to 1974, only three players in the majors collected more hits. The guy with the most was Pete Rose (left).

Alas, the Cards were snowed out, and the Bucs staged a miracle rally to wrap it up. For the second straight year, the division was lost while wearing street clothes.

Things got worse before they got better in the 1970s, the Cardinals hitting bottom in 1978 when they won 69 and lost 93. Amid that debacle, Busch fired off a scathing letter to the team in which he scolded, "The only way it is going to work out is with actions, and not words, with desire and dedication, not careless play and lackadaisical attitudes, and with some old-fashioned Cardinals Gashouse Gang spirit and guts."

Over the next three years, Busch rifled through five managers. One of them veritably oozed spirit and guts, and hunkered down to coerce and cajole the Cardinals into not only changing the way they played the game but also altering the very culture of their organization. Enter "Whiteyball."

It took 25 innings (seven hours and four minutes) for the Cards to shake the Mets on September 11, 1974. Only about 1,500 fans remained to see the game conclude at 3:13 A.M. The teams combined to use 180 baseballs, send 202 hitters to the plate, and leave a record 45 men on base.

WALL-TO-WALL CARPETING

The players didn't know it when they stepped onto Busch Stadium's new playing surface in 1970, but the synthetic AstroTurf—then four years into its existence—would come to define an entire era of Cardinals style and success. The hard, bouncy material amped up the game considerably. Balls quickly scooted to, and often past, defenders, while speedy runners bounced around the bases. In 1977, even the infield at Busch was blanketed with the stuff, leaving dirt only in the sliding areas. Artificial surfaces trended throughout baseball in the 1970s, and the number of stolen bases soared by nearly 50 percent during the decade. By the 1980s, the Cardinals would stand as Exhibit A in the game's newest evolution.

The installation of speed-friendly AstroTurf at Busch Stadium for the 1970 season triggered a go-go era of Cardinals baseball. Over the next two decades, no team would steal more bases—or hit fewer home runs.

Simba, the All-Star Catcher

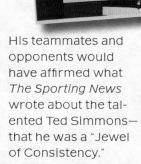

With his cascading locks that earned him the sobriquet "Simba" and his articulate oratory, Ted Simmons fit no stereotype of the crusty, crew cut, tobacco-spittin' backstop. "He didn't sound like a baseball player," pitcher Dan Quisenberry once noted. "He said things like 'nevertheless' and 'if, in fact.'" He also broke the mold for catchers when it came to durability (only one catcher has had more than his 13 straight 100-game seasons, though Simmons did not catch every one of those games), switch-hitting (none have matched his RBI, hits, or home runs), and, unhappily, surety of hands (he holds the modern NL record for passed balls).

Simmons was baseball's sole catcher to average above .300 during the 1970s, and he flexed enough muscle to be bested in home runs and RBI during that period by only

His teammates and opponents would have affirmed what *The Sporting News* wrote about the talented Ted Simmons—that he was a "Jewel of Consistency."

Ted Simmons has more hits than any catcher in the Hall of Fame, but he remains a fringe candidate. Not only does he lack a World Series ring, but more critically, Johnny Bench overshadowed him in his own era.

Johnny Bench. He landed the first six of his eight All-Star Game invitations while with St. Louis, and his 193 hits in 1975 are still tied for fourth by a player at his position.

Simmons's toughness, vocal audacity, and sharp intellect made him a favorite of his pitchers. On a corporate level, the same traits sometimes worked against him. Never reaching the postseason in his 13 years as a Cardinal exasperated him, and he was not shy about saying so. Trying to lighten the mood after one disheartening loss, he inflamed manager Vern Rapp into a tantrum by playing loud music in the clubhouse. Nine days later, Rapp was fired. The decision went the other way when old-school taskmaster Whitey Herzog, who considered Simmons a nuisance and a defensive liability, took over as manager/general manager in 1980. Weeks after winning the inaugural Silver Slugger Award for catcher, Ted was dealt to Milwaukee, where he lost to his old mates in the 1982 World Series despite hitting two home runs. In 1988, the Cardinals hired him as their farm director, after which he became general manager of the Pirates.

"All you ever hear is Bench and [Thurman] Munson and [Carlton] Fisk," said Pittsburgh manager Chuck Tanner in 1978. "Nobody ever talks about Simmons. He's the most underrated catcher. He's never got the recognition he deserves." Three decades and a few tractionless grassroots Hall of Fame campaigns later, he still doesn't.

Bake McBride tallied the tie-breaking run in the 25th inning of this 1974 marathon when he steamed to third base on an errant pickoff attempt and then scored when the Mets catcher missed a throw to the plate.

IT WAS HEADLINE NEWS WHEN LOU BROCK FINALLY BROKE TY COBB'S STOLEN BASE RECORD.

JOE TORRE'S BEST SEASON IN ST. LOUIS CAME IN 1971, WHEN HE WAS NAMED THE NL'S MOST VALUABLE PLAYER AFTER LEADING THE LEAGUE WITH A .363 AVERAGE, 137 RBI, 230 HITS, AND 352 TOTAL BASES. TORRE WAS THE FIRST PLAYER TO LEAD THE NATIONAL LEAGUE IN FOUR OFFENSIVE CATEGORIES SINCE STAN MUSIAL IN 1948.

ST. LOUIS POST-DISPATCH

FINAL
★★★
2:30 P.M. New York Stock
Pages 13A and 14A

On Today's Editorial Page
The March Of The Desert
Editorial
Two New Industries
Editorial

TUESDAY, AUGUST 30, 1977

15¢

VOL. 99   NO. 239   Copyright 1977, St. Louis Post-Dispatch

Tops Ty Cobb

Brock Steals Base No. 893

By DICK KAEGEL
Of the Post-Dispatch Staff

SAN DIEGO, Calif., Aug. 30 — Lou Brock had just broken Ty Cobb's record by stealing the 893rd base in his distinguished baseball career. The game was stopped while Brock was mobbed by his teammates. Pitcher Randy Jones, representing the San Diego Padres, presented second base to the Cardinals' star.

"It has not been an easy thing but the moment is here," Brock said into the field microphone. Then he grinned. "Looking back on it, Randy, I did it my way."

Indeed he did. And Brock's way was built on a rare combination of speed, style, cunning and the ability to stay cool under pressure. Faster runners have played the game, but Brock made basestealing an art. And, last night at San

PRAISE POURED in last night for new stolen base king Lou Brock. Page 4B
AMADEE looks at Lou Brock and Ty Cobb. Picture Page 1C

Diego Stadium, he executed his masterpiece.

Brock entered the game with 891 steals, needing two to surpass Cobb, the snarling hellcat who starred for the Detroit Tigers early in the century. Cobb had stolen his 892nd base 49 years ago, on Sept. 11, 1928, as he closed out his career with the Philadelphia Athletics.

Brock wasted no time last night. Batting first for the Cardinals, he began the game by drawing a walk on a three-

See BROCK, Page 5

THE BROCK LEGEND: Cardinal Lou Brock holding high the base he stole to set a new record as Manager Vern Rapp and others congratulated him (left). Below, Brock taking off from first in the seventh inning to set the record. The pitcher is Dave Freisleben of the San Diego Padres. Below, left, Brock sliding in toward baseball legend. (Post-Dispatch Photos by Jim Forbes)

THE 1970 ST. LOUIS CARDINALS SOUVENIR YEARBOOK FEATURED FUTURE HALL-OF-FAME PLAYERS SUCH AS BOB GIBSON, STEVE CARLTON, AND LOU BROCK.

Baseball

Garry Templeton

BOB FORSCH

NO-HITTER

WHITEWASHING THE PHILADELPHIA PHILLIES 5-0, ST. LOUIS CARDINAL RIGHT-HANDER BOB FORSCH PITCHED THE FIRST NO-HITTER OF HIS CAREER. HE WALKED ONLY TWO BATTERS, AND THE CARDINALS COMMITTED ONE ERROR. CATCHER—TED SIMMONS

SAINT LOUIS, MO APR 16 1978 63155

THIS GARRY TEMPLETON BASEBALL CARD IS FROM THE 1978 SPORTSCASTER SERIES, WHICH SHOWS HIM AS A ST. LOUIS CARDINAL. BUT HE WILL BE REMEMBERED FOR ALL TIME AS THE PLAYER THE CARDINALS TRADED TO SAN DIEGO TO ACQUIRE OZZIE SMITH.

BOB FORSCH, SHOWN ON THIS COMMEMORATIVE ENVELOPE, THREW THE FIRST NO-HITTER IN BUSCH STADIUM HISTORY ON APRIL 16, 1978, BEATING THE PHILLIES 5-0. THE NO-HITTER WAS PRESERVED WITH A DECISION BY THE OFFICIAL SCORER TO CHARGE THIRD BASEMAN KEN REITZ WITH AN ERROR INSTEAD OF GIVING GARRY MADDOX A HIT ON A HARD GROUNDER LEADING OFF THE EIGHTH INNING.

THE SUCCESS THE CARDINALS ENJOYED IN THE 1960S FAILED TO CONTINUE IN THE 1970S. THE FRANCHISE REGULARLY FELL SHORT OF THE PLAYOFFS IN THAT DECADE, THREE TIMES COMING AWAY WITH A SECOND-PLACE FINISH. THIS 1974 CARDINAL MEDIA GUIDE NOTES THEIR SECOND-PLACE FINISH IN 1973, ONLY A GAME AND A HALF BEHIND THE METS.

Eccentric but Effective

The winter after lefty Steve Carlton's first 20-win season in 1971, he was traded to the Phillies for Rick Wise. After he left, "Lefty" amassed 252 victories; meanwhile, Wise earned 32 for the Redbirds.

Steve Carlton's manners often were as unpardonable as his slider was unhittable. While with St. Louis from 1965 to 1971, he was an equal-opportunity jerk, consistently discourteous and boorish to fans, the front office, and everyone in between. (For the last 20 years of his career, he wouldn't speak to the sports media at all.) Between the lines, "Lefty" obviously channeled the nuances of his maverick personality to his advantage, arguably being the best left-handed pitcher who ever lived.

Because Gussie Busch considered him "a smart-aleck young guy," Carlton was an ex-Cardinal by age 27. That was still enough time in red and white for him to win 74 games in his five complete seasons and to make the first three of his ten All-Star rosters. The four-time Cy Young Award honoree pitched for another 17 years, accruing more victories than any southpaw other than Warren Spahn and more strikeouts than any save Randy Johnson.

Carlton was impenetrable—a one-time gawky and insecure youth who found sanctuary and success in Eastern religion, isometrics, martial arts, and visualization techniques. It wouldn't be hard to visualize several more Cardinals championships had he not been traded.

THE MAD HUNGARIAN

If Carlton's intensity simmered and seethed, Al Hrabosky's was overtly worn as a badge of honor. Before each pitch, the reliever would stalk to the back of the mound, meditate to a ferocious focus apparently on some unspeakable global cataclysm, return with a strut, and uncork a blazing fastball. The ritual not only made "The Mad Hungarian" a premier closer but also one of the team's most popular players ever. In 1974 and 1975, he went 21–4, with his 22 saves leading the NL in the latter year.

When, in 1977, manager Vern Rapp demanded Hrabosky's frightening furry Fu Manchu be shorn, the left-hander protested: "How can I intimidate batters if I look like a goddamn golf pro?" That bit of insurgency got him traded, but in 1985 Al was reincarnated as a broadcaster in St. Louis, where he still works as one of the team's TV sports announcers.

Above: When Al Hrabosky was overlooked for the 1974 All-Star Team, he was feted to a "We Hlove Hrabosky Hbanner Hday." He showed his happreciation the next season with the third-lowest ERA (1.66) ever by a Cardinals reliever.

Forsch Gets It Done

Although Bob Forsch is the only Cardinal to throw two no-hitters, he was more steady than sensational. "Forschie" seemed to raise his game at Busch Stadium, where he compiled a 93–60 career record.

Sabermetricians, the guardians of baseball's statistical secrets, keep Bob Forsch locked away in their analytical closets. He gave up too many hits, walked too many batters, struck out too few, and threw too many pitches to plausibly keep his team in as many ballgames and win as many times as he did.

The right-hander started 401 games for the Cardinals (more than anyone except Bob Gibson), going 163–127 from 1974 to 1988, yet his only awards were a couple of Silver Sluggers. "Effectively wild" as a power pitcher early in his career, he came to rely almost exclusively on well-placed sinkers and changeups.

One secret to Forsch's inconspicuous success was his ultimate-fighter tenacity. Catcher Darrell Porter called him "one of the greatest competitors you could ever find … very smart … not afraid of any hitter." Another was his stone-cold consistency; he was in his tenth season before he had a season ERA touch 4.00.

In his book, *Tales from the Cardinals Dugout*, Forsch wrote that St. Louis "will always be home. All of my life-long dreams were fulfilled here." Then, he added, "I think the fans probably remember me as better than I was." Even if the statisticians don't.

AT TIMES, UNHITTABLE

There were days when Forsch could place the ball to any spot around the plate as if it were laser-guided, inducing batter after batter to poke balls lamely to his fielders. He threw 19 shutouts, two of which were no-hitters. The first—tainted, some say, by an eighth-inning scoring decision—came against the Phillies on April 16, 1978, with Forsch striking out only three men. It was the first no-no by a Cardinal on their home field since Jesse Haines had spun one 54 years earlier.

BOB GIBSON PLAYED HIS ENTIRE CAREER WITH THE ST. LOUIS CARDINALS FROM 1959 TO 1975. HE IS ONE OF ONLY A FEW PITCHERS IN THE SECOND HALF OF THE 20TH CENTURY TO ENTER THE HALL OF FAME WITH AN ERA UNDER 3.00. HIS CAREER ERA IS 2.91.

BOB GIBSON
St. Louis Cardinals

ON AUGUST 14, 1971, BOB GIBSON PITCHED THE ONLY NO-HITTER OF HIS CAREER, DEFEATING THE PIRATES 11-0 AT THREE RIVERS STADIUM. THE BALLPARK IS PICTURED ON THE COVER OF THIS 1971 PIRATES SCOREBOOK.

Pittsburgh Pirates Official Scorebook 1971

THREE RIVERS STADIUM

35c

NEARLY 35 YEARS AFTER THE END OF HIS PLAYING CAREER IN 1975, BOB GIBSON STILL HOLDS THE CARDINALS' FRANCHISE RECORDS FOR MOST CAREER WINS, INNINGS PITCHED, STRIKEOUTS, COMPLETE GAMES, SHUTOUTS, AND BASES ON BALLS.

LOU BROCK MOVED INTO
SELECT COMPANY AMONG
BASEBALL'S IMMORTALS ON
AUGUST 13, 1979, WHEN HE
LINED A SINGLE OFF THE
HAND OF THE CUBS' DENNIS
LAMP AND REACHED FIRST
WITHOUT A PLAY—THE 3,000TH
HIT OF HIS CAREER. HE RETIRED
AFTER THAT SEASON WITH 3,023 CAREER HITS.

ON AUGUST 29, 1977, LOU BROCK STOLE THE
893RD BASE OF HIS CAREER AGAINST THE
PADRES, PASSING TY COBB FOR THE MOST
STOLEN BASES IN MODERN HISTORY. RICKEY
HENDERSON HAS SINCE BROKEN BROCK'S
RECORD.

BOB GIBSON WAS ONE OF THE
BEST-HITTING PITCHERS OF ALL
TIME. IN 1970, HE EVEN BATTED .303,
COLLECTING 33 HITS. AND AS GREAT
AS HIS PITCHING WAS IN THE 1967 WORLD SERIES, HE ALSO
CLOBBERED A HOMER. AMAZINGLY, HE HOMERED FIVE TIMES IN 1972 AT AGE 36.

CHAPTER SIX

SPEED BALL
1980–1989

THE STORMY 1970S mercifully gave way to the entertaining 1980s as St. Louis fans were bombarded with W's: Whiteyball, The Wiz, Willie—and wins. With Whitey Herzog unleashing his innovative brand of swaggering, speed-saturated baseball, the Cardinals narrative grew by three pennants and one world championship.

When Whitey Herzog, shown on this silk cachet, was named manager of the Cardinals in June 1980, expectations of fans were high. Just two years later, however, few predicted the team would be world champions and Herzog named "Man of the Year" by *The Sporting News*.

Left: "Whiteyball" bestowed upon the Cards a winning personality. Whitey Herzog, however, could be tough to play for. "If [my players] need a buddy," he spat, "let them buy a dog."

Right: The arrival of shortstop Ozzie Smith helped vault the Redbirds into the 1982 World Series against Milwaukee, the first of three fall classic trips during the decade.

SPORTING NEWS
MAN OF THE YEAR

Jackie Robinson

SAINT LOUIS
JAN
20
1983
63155

WHITEY HERZOG

FOR HIS FINE MANAGING OF THE ST. LOUIS CARDINALS IN 1982 WHITEY HERZOG WAS NAMED SPORTING NEWS MAN OF THE YEAR ON JANUARY 30, 1983. IN THE SHORT TIME BETWEEN 1980 AND 1982 HERZOG GUIDED THE CARDS UP FROM THE DEPTHS OF MEDIOCRITY TO THE HEIGHT OF SUPREMACY AS HE LED THEM TO THE 1982 WORLD CHAMPIONSHIP OVER THE HIGHLY FAVORED MILWAUKEE BREWERS.

The Wizard

Of all the trades made by Herzog in turning the Cardinals from a mediocre club into a multi-pennant winner, perhaps no deal was more important than trading Garry Templeton to the San Diego Padres for Ozzie Smith, whose defense is extolled on this figurine.

OZZIE SMITH "Defense"

To anyone who would listen, manager Whitey Herzog would assert that Ozzie Smith "saves more than 100 runs a year with his glove." Hyperbole or no, the incomparable shortstop saved something more imperative: the Cardinals' reputation as an elite franchise. Following a mediocre, monochromatic 1970s decade, Smith arrived in 1982 to reinstate shades of zest, charisma, identity, and urgency to the team. And with those qualities came the restoration of a winning tradition.

Ozzie was the essence of the 1980s Cardinals, a team built to exploit the vast dimensions and racetrack turf of Busch Memorial Stadium. It seemed his feet barely skimmed the ground at shortstop as he redrew the borders of range for the position, pouncing down and bouncing up for throw-'em-outs seemingly outside the range of human athletic capacity. Offensively, Smith gave no quarter to his wispy build, compensating by teaching himself a slap-and-scoot hitting style, precision bat-handling, and the finer points of base thievery.

The upshot was a position-record 13 Gold Gloves, 15 All-Star Game appearances, 2,460 hits, 580 stolen bases, 214 sacrifice

Ozzie Smith performed his extemporaneous defensive ballet in St. Louis throughout the 1980s and well into the 1990s, almost single-handedly returning the franchise to relevance. "He plays," said teammate Andy Van Slyke, "like he's wearing helium kangaroo shorts."

bunts, countless run-building situational executions, a Silver Slugger Award in a year he went homerless, and ultimately a niche in Cooperstown. "The Wizard of Oz"—or "Ahhs"—is still the all-time assists leader and the NL record-holder for double plays at his position.

Consensus says there has never been a better defensive shortstop than Smith—or a more respected one. The fans worshipped him, eager to buy a ticket if just to witness a no-hands backflip en route to his position. His teammates drew strength from him. "He meant everything," said catcher Darrell Porter. "He was a leader in the clubhouse. He was a guy who demanded other people do their best, that they play for the team."

During his illustrious career, Smith won the Lou Gehrig, Branch Rickey, Roberto Clemente, and NCAA Image awards for off-field contributions. He remains an ambassador of the game through his charitable endeavors and inspirational speeches. "I sincerely believe," he said at his Hall of Fame induction in 2002, "that there is nothing truly great in any man or woman except their character, their willingness to move beyond the realm of self and into a greater realm of selflessness. Giving back is the ultimate talent in life. That is the greatest trophy on my mantel."

But there is still one piece of unfinished business between Ozzie Smith and the Cardinals. In 1996, his farewell season, a public feud mushroomed between him and Tony La Russa over playing time. "I don't want to be anywhere he is," La Russa was still insisting a decade later. Smith, in turn, has distanced himself from the organization until "things change, when management changes … [but] I know it's where I belong. That time will come."

Ozzie Smith thrilled fans with his customary backflips on opening day each year and before the first game of a postseason series.

Whitey's Way

To owner Gussie Busch, Whitey Herzog reflected the Cardinals roster he inherited as manager/general manager in 1980 as a wretched collection of malingerers, prima donnas, drug addicts, alcoholics, egomaniacs, and unathletic ninnies. Out came the broom. Within three years, he turned over more than half of his batting order and almost the entire pitching staff.

The new Cardinals were reconstituted with the formula that won Herzog three division titles with the Kansas City Royals, another team with a spacious turf park. His wish list: pitchers who wanted the ball, a fearless stopper in the pen, defenders who could eat up ground, selfless contact hitters to exploit the gaps and move runners, and players who could run—and run through walls to win. His modus operandi: Hit the ball on the ground, bunt, steal (a lot), take the extra base, catch the baseball, build a lead, and hand over the game to your closer.

It was a brilliant blueprint, exquisitely executed. From 1981 to 1989, with "The White Rat" as skipper, the Cards won more games than any team in the National League, three pennants, and a World Series. "Whiteyball," as it was dubbed in the sports media, was more than a fashion of play; it was a baseball revolution.

The World Series trophy returned to St. Louis in 1982, for the first time in 15 years. The presentation was made by commissioner Bowie Kuhn (left) to Whitey Herzog (right) with owner August Busch and NBC broadcaster Bob Costas looking on.

Cards Pound the Wallbangers

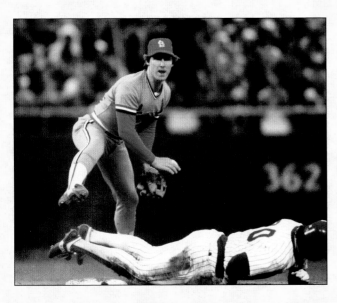

Above: Tom Herr, here making a relay over Milwaukee's Gorman Thomas in the 1982 Series, turned the third-most double plays (730) and posted the second-highest fielding percentage (.988) ever by a Cardinals second-sacker.

Right: Celebrants met at the mound as the Cardinals wrapped the 1982 World Series.

Perhaps never in its history has a World Series featured teams with such polarized prescriptions for success as in 1982. It was the one-base-at-a-time, defense-stressing tack of Whitey Herzog's Cardinals versus the brute, ball-bashing assault of Harvey Kuenn's Milwaukee Brewers. St. Louis's top two basestealers had more stolen bags than the entire Milwaukee roster. The Brew Crew's top two home run hitters had more dingers than the entire Cardinals roster. Fans of both squads geared up to watch the grand diametric struggle between "Whiteyball" and "Harvey's Wallbangers" unfold.

St. Louis, which had swept Atlanta in the NL Championship Series, was staggered, 10–0, in the Series opener. In Game 2, catcher Darrell Porter, often scorned by Cards fans who resented the trade of Ted Simmons (now with the Brewers), keyed a 5–4 equalizer by cuffing two key hits and gunning down a runner in the ninth.

It was all Willie McGee in the third game, as the Cards' center fielder slugged two home runs and robbed Milwaukee of a pair of extra-base hits with circus catches. The Brewers answered with a Game 4 comeback fueled by three unearned runs. After another loss, the Cardinals faced elimination as they returned to Busch, where they recovered with some wallbanging of their own: a 13–1 coast behind John Stuper's four-hitter. Playing a Game 7 for the eighth time in franchise history, St. Louis ran its record to 7–1, prevailing 6–3. Despite McGee's heroics, two saves and a win by Sutter, and eight RBI from Hernandez, Porter was named the Series MVP.

"They called it 'Whiteyball' and said it couldn't last," Herzog reveled. It was just getting started.

THE GREAT INJUSTICE

The taste of the great injustice of 1981 still lingers in St. Louis like a rancid bratwurst. For the only time in history, the team with the best record in its division was ineligible for the post-season. After a 50-day players' strike, the owners voted to send the divisional winners from each "half" of the season to the playoffs. The Cards, 59–43 overall, finished a close second in each segment—and went home for the winter.

EVEN THOUGH WHITEY HERZOG DECIDED THAT THE CARDINALS HAD TO TRADE GARRY TEMPLETON, FEATURED IN THIS SPORTS MAGAZINE, HE WAS DETERMINED NOT TO JUST GIVE HIM AWAY. THE ONLY SHORTSTOPS HERZOG THOUGHT WERE EQUAL TO TEMPLETON WERE ALAN TRAMMELL, IVAN DEJESUS, RICK BURLESON, AND OZZIE SMITH.

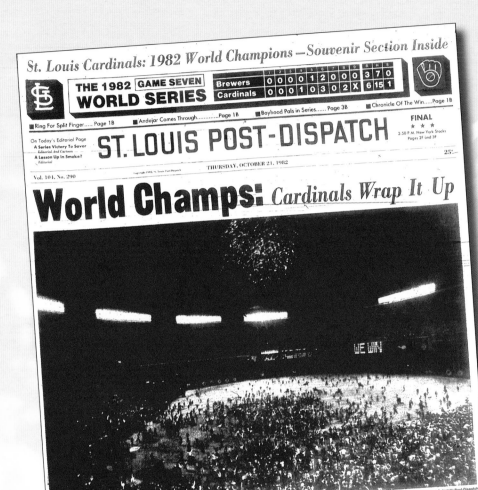

WINNING A BASEBALL WORLD CHAMPIONSHIP IS ALWAYS HEADLINE NEWS AND A GREAT REASON TO CELEBRATE.

FOR THE FIRST TIME SINCE 1968, THE CARDINALS MADE IT BACK TO THE WORLD SERIES IN 1982. THIS PROGRAM FEATURES THE TWO CLUBS IN THAT WORLD SERIES— THE MILWAUKEE BREWERS AND THE ST. LOUIS CARDINALS, WHOSE CATCHER, DARRELL PORTER, WAS NAMED THE MVP OF THE SERIES.

THE 1985 WORLD SERIES BETWEEN THE CARDINALS AND ROYALS WAS DUBBED THE "I-70 SERIES" IN HONOR OF THE INTERSTATE HIGHWAY THAT RUNS ACROSS MISSOURI BETWEEN ST. LOUIS AND KANSAS CITY. BECAUSE WHITEY HERZOG STILL MADE HIS OFF-SEASON HOME IN INDEPENDENCE, MISSOURI, HE JOKED THAT HE GOT TO SLEEP IN HIS OWN BED EVERY NIGHT.

THE CARDINALS' SUCCESSFUL TEAMS IN THE 1980S PLAYED A BRAND OF BASEBALL QUICKLY DUBBED "WHITEYBALL," FEATURING TEAMS THAT HAD LITTLE POWER BUT COMBINED HITTING FOR AVERAGE, STEALING BASES, AND GREAT DEFENSE TO WIN THREE PENNANTS IN SIX SEASONS.

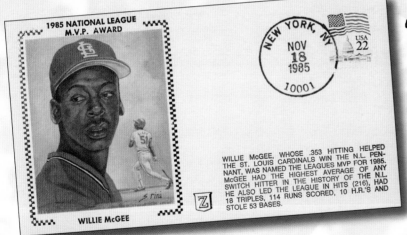

1985 NATIONAL LEAGUE M.V.P. AWARD

WILLIE McGEE

WILLIE McGEE, WHOSE .353 HITTING HELPED THE ST. LOUIS CARDINALS WIN THE N.L. PENNANT, WAS NAMED THE LEAGUES MVP FOR 1985. McGEE HAD THE HIGHEST AVERAGE OF ANY SWITCH HITTER IN THE HISTORY OF THE N.L. HE ALSO LED THE LEAGUE IN HITS (216), HAD 18 TRIPLES, 114 RUNS SCORED, 10 H.R.'S AND STOLE 53 BASES.

WILLIE MCGEE, SHOWN ON THIS SILK CACHET, WAS NAMED THE NATIONAL LEAGUE MVP IN 1985. HIS .353 BATTING AVERAGE LED THE LEAGUE AND WAS THE HIGHEST IN MODERN NL HISTORY FOR A SWITCH-HITTER. THE ONLY CARDINAL SINCE 1948 TO HAVE MORE THAN HIS 216 HITS IN A SEASON WAS JOE TORRE IN 1971 WITH 230.

THE CARDINALS' CHANCES OF WINNING THE 1987 WORLD SERIES WERE HURT BY THE LOSS OF INJURED PLAYERS JACK CLARK AND TERRY PENDLETON. THE TEAM ULTIMATELY WOUND UP JUST SHORT, LOSING THE DECIDING SEVENTH GAME TO THE TWINS AT THE METRODOME.

Cardinals Thunder...

In the 1980s, 103 players in baseball hit 100 or more home runs. None did so wearing a Cardinals uniform. George Hendrick, with 89, came the closest. Though a stone-faced enigma to fans because of his utter silence (a teammate once speculated George didn't even talk to his wife), colleagues were keen on his outfield excellence and knack for driving in big runs. From 1978 to 1984, he was far and away the club's home run and RBI leader.

When Dal Maxvill took over as GM after the 1984 season, his first big trade sent Hendrick to the Pirates for pitching ace-to-be John Tudor. He then replaced his cleanup hitter with first baseman Jack Clark from the Giants. Those moves begat two pennants. Free agency claimed "Jack the Ripper" after only three seasons, but he was the most feared Cardinals masher since Stan Musial. He contributed 57 homers and 193 RBI total to the 1985 and 1987 NL crowns. When Clark was hurt most of 1986, the Cardinals plummeted to 79–82.

Far less imposing, but no less significant, was Tommy Herr. The regular second baseman from 1981 to 1987, Herr modeled what Whitey Herzog wanted in a ballplayer: an overachieving switch-hitter with a preternatural sense for what it took to win a ballgame. In 1985, he was (and still is) the only player since World War II to drive in as many as 110 runs with as few as eight homers.

Athletically, Jack Clark was a mule in a stable of Cardinals thoroughbreds, but one with a vigorous kick. Almost one out of every three home runs hit by the 1985 and 1987 pennant-winners came off his bat.

George Hendrick treated the sports media like a disease, but he was also a pox on pitchers. He played for 18 seasons with six teams, but his two Silver Slugger Awards (one each as an outfielder and first baseman) came while wearing the "birds on the bat."

...and Lightning

Classy Cardinal Willie McGee was a painful perfectionist as a center fielder and was very popular with the Cardinals fans. "He looks like he doesn't have a friend in the world," announcer Jack Buck once said. "Meanwhile, all the world is his friend."

Outfielders Willie McGee, Lonnie Smith, and Vince Coleman weren't perfect. The scrawny, pigeon-toed McGee always looked as if he were in pain; Smith, called "Skates" for his defensive misadventures, battled substance abuse; and Coleman missed much of the 1985 postseason because of an injury he sustained when his leg got caught under a tarp he had not noticed prior to an NLCS game. But with their unadulterated, unprecedented, unstoppable speed, they were perfect for Whiteyball. Together they accounted for 1,023 stolen bases in St. Louis.

McGee and Smith were acquired in trades—for almost nothing—within a month of each other after the 1981 season. Coleman came up through the system and was Rookie of the Year as Smith's replacement in 1985. Willie was the most accomplished of the trio. He won an MVP Award, three Gold Gloves, and a couple of batting titles while helping the club into the postseason four times. "Vincent van Go" was the master thief, topping 100 steals during each of his first three years.

"Teams hated coming in here playing on those hot

summer days," said Ozzie Smith, another Cardinal who scorched the Busch turf with 433 swipes of his own.

Vince Coleman kicked up a storm of stolen bases, leading the league in each of his six St. Louis seasons. After he left, he kicked up storms of controversy by recklessly hurting Dwight Gooden's arm with a golf club, injuring three people when he lobbed a lit firecracker into a crowd of fans, and professing ignorance of Jackie Robinson's legacy.

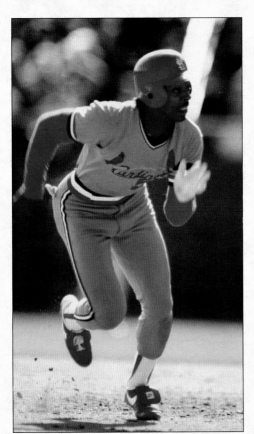

WILLIE McGEE, MVP

The endearing McGee's baseball smarts, unselfish play, and humble, generous character could not be quantified, but in 1985, his stats added up to an NL MVP Award. The earnest, worrywart center fielder catalyzed a pennant winner with his .353 average (a modern NL record for a switch-hitter), 56 stolen bases, 54 extra-base hits, 82 RBI, and graceful, ground-gobbling defense. Still, his was the kind of detail-oriented, win-producing performance that only an eyewitness could fully appreciate. "I'd like to think he made us better players," said reserve outfielder John Morris. "In the long run, it made us better people."

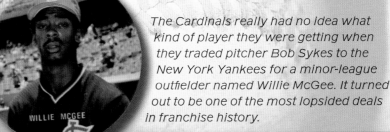

The Cardinals really had no idea what kind of player they were getting when they traded pitcher Bob Sykes to the New York Yankees for a minor-league outfielder named Willie McGee. It turned out to be one of the most lopsided deals in franchise history.

WILLIE McGEE

The "Show Me" World Series

Without a doubt, 1985 was a "Show Me" season. The Cardinals first showed they were not the same team that played barely break-even ball the previous two years by fielding their only 100-win club from 1968 to 2003. It was "Whiteyball" at its apex, as St. Louis led the NL in runs (despite ranking 11th in homers) and fielding and was second in ERA.

For the first two games of the NLCS, the Cardinals didn't show up—their twin 20-game winners, John Tudor and Joaquin Andujar, were rocked by the Dodgers. Back at Busch, they evened the series to set the stage for a pair of classics. With Game 5 tied 2–2 in the ninth, the voice of Jack Buck relieved millions of anxious radio listeners: "Go crazy, folks! Go crazy! It's a home run." The impossible hero was Ozzie Smith, poling his first long ball as a lefty hitter after more than 3,000 at-bats. Jack Clark provided more ninth-inning histrionics—and the pennant—with a game-winning three-run homer in the next game.

That set up a "Show Me" World Series against the neighboring Kansas City Royals. A Tudor shutout in Game 4 put the Cardinals within one game of a ring, but things deteriorated quickly as they dropped three straight—one routinely, one amid controversy, and one in abject humiliation (see sidebar).

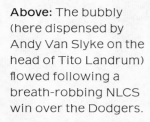

Above: The bubbly (here dispensed by Andy Van Slyke on the head of Tito Landrum) flowed following a breath-robbing NLCS win over the Dodgers.

Right: The 1985 World Series meltdown was a team effort, but it's often symbolized by Joaquin Andujar (here restrained by coach Nick Leyva after his ejection). His histrionics carried over to the clubhouse in an ugly scene involving a bat and a toilet.

THAT DANG DENKINGER!

If "Denkinger" is not technically a curse word, it cannot be uttered in St. Louis without preceding it with one. Umpire Don Denkinger's "safe" call of a replay-confirmed out at first base in Game 6 probably cost the Cards the 1985 Series. The gaffe opened the door to a two-run bottom-of-the-ninth Royals rally as St. Louis lost its 1–0 lead. What followed was a chain of misplays and then a ghastly 11–0 meltdown in Game 7. The team that almost certainly was the Cardinals' best of the 1980s had dissolved into a historical footnote.

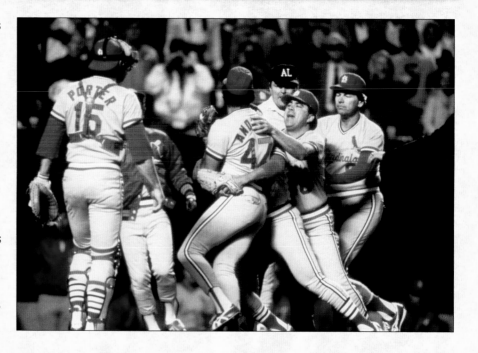

Done In by the Twins

them out in Games 1, 2, and 6, and then Minnesota mustered a comeback in the finale to complete the upset.

The 1987 World Series, called "The Series on the Mississippi" because of the two cities' location on its riverbank, was the first to include indoor games and the first in which the home teams went unbeaten. And although a team with the worst regular-season record (85–77) of any champ up to that time dumped the Cardinals, they would one day exact a measure of vindication. The 2006 world-champion Redbirds were a mere 83–78.

Left: With Jack Clark limited to one at-bat in the 1987 postseason, the Cardinals turned to midseason pickup Dan Driessen as a platoon first baseman.

Below: Tommy Herr's last hurrah came in the 1987 Series. He was traded the following spring to the Twins, the very team that beat out the Cards for the world championship.

Whiteyball suffered a blackout in 1986 as the Cards went from first to worst in the league in scoring, but the next season brought a revival of the team's swashbuckling ways. Despite losing 35 of their last 69 outings, they survived a tight NL East race and a seven-game NLCS with the Giants.

St. Louis would have to confront the Minnesota Twins in the World Series without their fulcrum, however; Jack Clark had torn an ankle tendon. As it turned out, offense was the least of the Cardinals' problems, as their rotation averaged fewer than five innings per start and compiled a 6.55 ERA. St. Louis swept the middle three contests at Busch, but the Twins blew

Although the Cards fell short of defeating the Minnesota Twins in the 1987 World Series, the players and team officials received commemorative rings for winning the National League pennant.

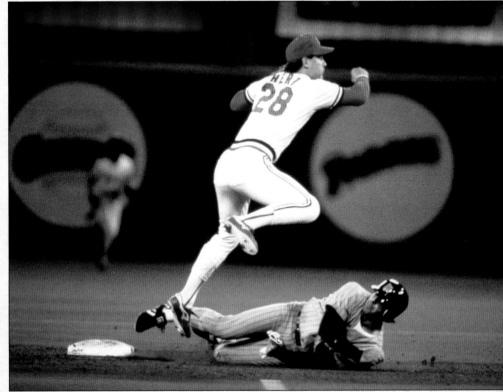

A Trio of Aces

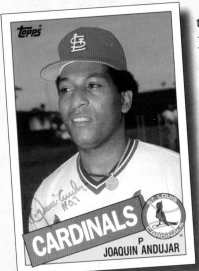

For each of their trio of titles in the 1980s, the Cards shuffled a different ace out of their pitching deck.

In 1982, it was Joaquin Andujar, the self-proclaimed "One Tough Dominican." The eccentric right-hander posted a 2.47 ERA, then won the third and seventh World Series games. Despite two 20-win seasons, he was traded when his ejection from Game 7 contributed to the 1985 World Series debacle. Andujar, despite the ungraceful exit, was a favorite who entertained not only with his pitching but also with his quotes ("There is one word in America that says it all … 'youneverknow'") and quirks (such as taking showers while clothed).

John Tudor's 1985 season is deemed the second-best ever by a Cardinal pitcher behind Bob Gibson's in 1968. The lefty started 1–7, then won 20 of his last 21 decisions (including 10 shutouts) to finish with a 1.93 ERA. Sore-armed and exhausted, Tudor won twice in the World Series before getting shelled in Game 7.

In the 1987 NLCS comeback against the Giants, St. Louis pitchers spun back-to-back shutouts to save the season. Danny Cox, a big changeup artist, won 41 games (and three more in the postseason) from 1985 to 1987 before hurting his elbow.

FORSCH'S SECOND NO-NO

Though not the sort of pitcher with "no-hit" stuff, Bob Forsch became the only Cardinals pitcher ever to throw two of them when he stymied the Expos at Busch Stadium on September 26, 1983, five years after his first. In his second no-hitter, the plucky righty was separated from a perfect game only by a hit batter and an error. Forsch admitted to occasionally doctoring the ball late in his career, but he maintained he did so legally. K-Y Jelly, he asserted, was made in the USA and therefore not a "foreign substance."

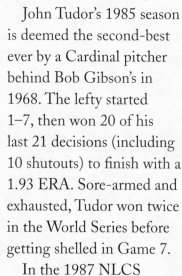

Top left: Despite his controversial personality, Joaquin Andujar remains the last Cardinal pitcher to win 20 or more games in consecutive years in 1984 and 1985. This 1985 sports card lists his remarkable pitching stats.

Bottom left: Danny Cox was a member of the starting rotation for the pennant-winning teams in 1985 and 1987.

Right: John Tudor beat the Royals twice in the 1985 fall classic, but he was disastrously ineffective in Game 7. His career 2.52 ERA and .705 winning percentage are Redbird records for pitchers with at least 100 starts.

Door Slammers

Bruce Sutter suited "Whiteyball" to a tee as the door-slammer in tight, low-scoring games. From 1981 to 1984, he amassed 35 more saves than any other closer in the National League, and in 28 percent of his opportunities he didn't even allow a baserunner.

Whiteyball will forever be defined in terms of speed, but Herzog knew that the races were won at the finish line. "My whole team was the preliminary act to Bruce Sutter's showstopper," he told Peter Golenbock in *The Spirit of St. Louis*.

Sutter was Herzog's stopper from 1981 to 1984, a period in which he led the league in saves three times. During the 1982 postseason, he won two games and saved three, including Game 7 of the World Series.

Blessed with enormous hands but cursed with elbow problems, Bruce perfected the so-called "pitch of the '80s"—the split-fingered fastball. In 2006, he became the first pitcher inducted into the Hall of Fame never to have started a game.

When the Cards lost Sutter to Atlanta as a free agent, they trotted out a successor who would be similarly "automatic." Todd Worrell tied a World Series record with six straight strikeouts in 1985,

yet was still technically a rookie in 1986, when he set a big-league record for freshmen with 36 saves.

More in the contemporary mold of the closer as a strapping fireballer, his unfortunate legacy in St. Louis is his blown save in Game 6 of the 1985 Series. But before being signed away in 1993, Worrell surpassed Sutter's team record for career saves.

Closer Todd Worrell had barely 30 innings of major-league experience when he failed (with "help" from Don Denkinger) to protect the Game 6 lead that would have secured the 1985 World Series.

OZZIE SMITH WON 13 CONSECUTIVE GOLD GLOVES DURING HIS HALL OF FAME CAREER. THE ONLY OTHER CARDINAL SHORTSTOPS TO WIN A GOLD GLOVE WERE DAL MAXVILL (1968) AND EDGAR RENTERIA (2002 AND 2003).

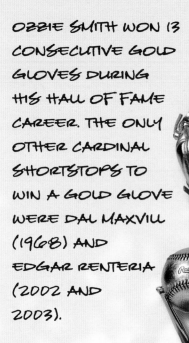

VINCE COLEMAN WAS CALLED UP FROM THE MINOR LEAGUES IN 1985 BECAUSE OF INJURIES TO WILLIE MCGEE AND TITO LADRUM. COLEMAN WAS EXPECTED TO STAY FOR ONLY A COUPLE OF WEEKS. INSTEAD HE STAYED FOR SIX YEARS BEFORE SIGNING WITH THE METS AS A FREE AGENT. DURING HIS YEARS WITH THE CARDS, HE WORE 29 ON HIS UNIFORM.

FOR THE 1985 SEASON, VINCE COLEMAN WAS NAMED ROOKIE OF THE YEAR. BEFORE THE FOLLOWING BASEBALL SEASON, HE AUTOGRAPHED SCORES OF BALLS LIKE THIS ONE FOR HIS MANY DEVOTED FANS. HIS 110 STEALS AS A ROOKIE ARE STILL A MAJOR-LEAGUE RECORD.

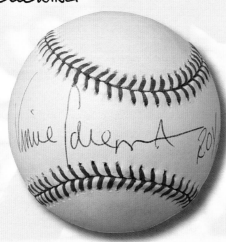

OZZIE SMITH IS ONE OF JUST NINE PLAYERS WHO HAVE HAD THEIR JERSEY NUMBER RETIRED BY THE CARDINALS. BEFORE OZZIE, POPULAR NUMBER 1 WAS WORN BY MANY CARDINALS, INCLUDING PEPPER MARTIN, WHITEY KUROWSKI, AND GARRY TEMPLETON.

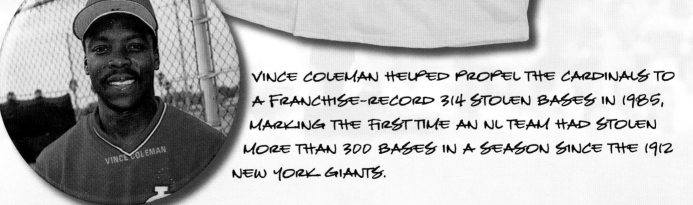

IN THE SAME GAME LATE IN THE 1985 SEASON, VINCE COLEMAN STOLE HIS 100TH BASE OF THE YEAR AND TOMMY HERR COLLECTED HIS 100TH RBI.

VINCE COLEMAN HELPED PROPEL THE CARDINALS TO A FRANCHISE-RECORD 314 STOLEN BASES IN 1985, MARKING THE FIRST TIME AN NL TEAM HAD STOLEN MORE THAN 300 BASES IN A SEASON SINCE THE 1912 NEW YORK GIANTS.

CHAPTER SEVEN

REDBIRD REVIVAL
1990–PRESENT

WITH THE END of the "Busch administration" came a period of, first, futility, then renewal. By the turn of the millennium, the Cardinals were again at the top of their game. Whereas the "Big Mac Attack" of the late 1990s was the spark, the winning fires weren't restoked until the arrival of Jim Edmonds, Scott Rolen, Jason Isringhausen, Chris Carpenter, and, especially, a young slugger called "Prince Albert."

Beginning in 1982, and with only two exceptions, the Cardinals drew two million or more fans to Busch Stadium every year until this ballpark's final season in 2005. The exceptions were 1994 (when the season was shortened because of a players' strike) and 1995 (revised shortened season). In fact, the attendance in nine of those seasons exceeded three million.

Right: The third iteration of Busch Stadium played host to an improbable championship season in its first year of operation. For the St. Louis Cardinals, *yesterday* had transitioned seamlessly into *today.*

Left: From 1997 to 2001, the Cardinals were all about the "Big Mac Attack." McGwire's larger-than-life persona, however, has since been tarnished by accusations of steroid use and his equivocal testimony to the U.S. Congress on the topic.

Loyalists Buy the Birds

After a 23-year absence, the World Series trophy was back in Cardinal hands in 2006. Accepting are, from left to right, Albert Pujols and his son, owner Bill DeWitt, general manager Walt Jocketty, and manager Tony La Russa.

August A. "Gussie" Busch, Jr., passed away late in the 1989 season, his 37th as franchise owner. Over the next few years, the beer company's enthusiasm for operating the club waned, and with it, performance on the field and at the turnstiles. In 1995, the team was sold. August Busch III—as had Fred Saigh—accepted much less ($150 million) than the team was worth to keep it in St. Louis. And if anyone deserved a hometown discount, it was this ownership group.

Redbirds roots ran deep for several of the principals. Bill DeWitt, Jr. (the majority owner), Fred Hanser, and Drew Baur were classmates at St. Louis Country Day School; they played youth baseball at Fairgrounds Park; and they regularly attended games together at Busch. DeWitt's dad rose from Cardinals office boy to owner of the Browns. (Bill was nine when little person Eddie Gaedel borrowed his uniform for that team's infamous 1951 publicity stunt!) Hanser's great grandfather was part-owner of the Cards from 1917 to 1947.

Their new asset came endowed with just one blue-chip holding: general manager Walt Jocketty, who was among the last hirings of the old regime. The GM had recently enlisted Tony La Russa as manager, and over the next decade, Jocketty's bold trade acquisitions would include Mark McGwire, Edgar Renteria, Jim Edmonds, Scott Rolen, and other critical gears in the team's winning mechanism. The Cardinals were staying in St. Louis, and they were finally going places.

SAD FAREWELLS

The emotional high of a 2002 season in which the Cardinals romped to the NL Central crown was interrupted by a tragic five days in June. On the 18th, Jack Buck, the team's broadcaster of 47 years, succumbed after an illness. The club staged a public viewing at home plate and engraved the initials "JFB" in the turf. Shockingly, on the 22nd, pitching ace Darryl Kile was found dead of natural causes. A grieving team rededicated itself and stretched a 2½-game lead into 13 in the final three months.

Above: All-Star Darryl Kile was a 36-game-winning ace in 2000 and 2001, a fan favorite, and a beloved teammate. Five days after his win over the Angels moved the Cards into first place in 2002, he was found dead of coronary disease at age 33.

Genius in the Dugout

There is no instruction book on how to be a major-league manager, but if there were, it would quite possibly be authored by Tony La Russa. The Cardinals skipper from 1996 to the present is one of the more complex and multifarious individuals ever to hold the job, and he's among the most successful.

The four-time Manager of the Year has been a field boss continuously for the White Sox, A's, and Cards since 1979, rising to third on the all-time wins list behind legends Connie Mack and John McGraw. He was a three-time pennant and 1989 World Series winner with Oakland. He then delivered six divisional titles, two NL crowns, and an improbable 2006 world championship to St. Louis. How he's done it is both art and science.

A weak-hitting major-league infielder at 18, La Russa earned his industrial management degree during his lengthy career in the minors, then passed the bar exam. At 34, he was a big-league skipper who quickly revealed himself as an idiosyncratic genius. He fastidiously manages (overmanages, say traditionalists) a pitching staff, coalesces computerized statistical analysis with a canny eye for talent, and alternately endears and alienates with his doctrinaire insistence on results at any price.

A new era of Cardinal baseball began in 1996 when Anheuser-Busch sold the ballclub. New owners took over, and Tony La Russa arrived from the Oakland A's to take over as the team's manager. Here is one of his lineup cards.

He is concurrently a combative autocrat and a fierce advocate for his players. Yet he has a soft enough touch outside the lines to be a vociferous activist for animal rights.

In *Men at Work*, author George Will perceives that La Russa "looks like an angry man, but he is not. He is, however, serious—about everything." The ballfield, after all, is Tony's courtroom, where he pleads his case, outwits his opponent, and manipulates the proceedings to gainful outcome. He is just the fifth lawyer to manage in the majors, following Monte Ward, Hughie Jennings, Branch Rickey, and Miller Huggins. The final baseball destination of each, as it will be for La Russa, was Cooperstown.

The many-sided Tony La Russa is a lawyer, the namesake of a popular video game, a subject of a best-selling book (*Men at Work* by George F. Will), a 2007 nominee for the "World's Sexiest Vegetarian," and the third-winningest manager in baseball history.

Big Mac Attack

McGwire was born two years to the day after Roger Maris hit his record 61st home run in 1961. Thirty-seven years later, Mac hit his 61st of the season on his father's 61st birthday.

There has never been a more commanding, or controversial, figure in Cardinals history than Mark McGwire. While locked in a monumental struggle with the Cubs' Sammy Sosa for home run supremacy in 1998, Mac's every mighty swing was an international incident. But because of his sad appearance at a U.S. congressional hearing concerning his involvement in baseball's steroid scandal, his place in MLB history has been questioned.

McGwire arrived from Oakland at the 1997 trading deadline with 24 of his season's 58 clouts still left in his bat. Once a lanky 6'5", he was by then, at 33, a statuesque behemoth. Jose Canseco, his former A's "Bash Brother," called him "an alien from the future who's come back to show us how to play the game."

In 1998, Big Mac vs. Slammin' Sammy was the feel-good summer blockbuster. Their congenial competition captivated as each chipped away at Roger Maris's hallowed home run record of 61 with breathtaking urgency. When the sport finally exhaled, McGwire had come away with 70, Sosa with 66—the first baseman's home runs traveling an otherworldly 5.6 miles in all.

Mac cleared 65 more fences in 1999, then retired in 2001, later to be implicated in Canseco's explosive book on steroid use. "I'm not here to discuss the past," an evasive McGwire repeatedly told the congressional committee in 2005 when asked if he'd used steroids. The phrase echoes as mournfully in St. Louis as "Say it ain't so, Joe" does in Chicago. Whether the mythical letter on McGwire's chest denotes Superman or the other S-word may remain an eternal debate. But there is no disputing that his legacy is a unique and exhilarating chapter in Cardinals annals, be it one of felicity or fraud.

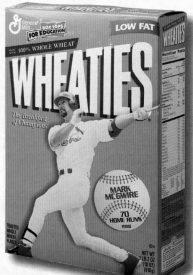

A trade with Oakland on July 31, 1997, brought Mark McGwire from the A's to the Cardinals. He immediately became one of the greatest home run hitters in franchise history, setting the stage for his historic 1998 season.

More Muscle Men

The triangulation of Scott Rolen at third base, Jim Edmonds in center field, and Albert Pujols at first has formed the nucleus of the 21st century Cardinals. One year at a time they arrived—Edmonds in a 2000 trade with the Angels, Pujols as an explosive 2001 rookie, and Rolen from Philadelphia the next summer. The decorated "Prince Albert" has been a Rookie of the Year, MVP, batting champ, Gold Glover, and multiple Silver-Slugger winner. The other two are Gold Glove "lifers" with imposing, if not quite Pujolsian, batting credentials.

It was no coincidence that the Cards improved by 20 wins when Edmonds showed up. He homered 42 times that season (one shy of Johnny Mize's team record for a lefty) and hit 168 more over the next five. In center, he has been known to vogue a routine catch into a photo op, but he's also routinely spectacular, offering up his well-being to the gods of ERA with full-sprint lunges and wince-inducing bellyflops.

"You're the best player I've ever been around," Tony La Russa once told Pujols. The statement would have been unsurprising from anyone who's watched the still-young superstar mock the record books with upward of a .300 average, 30 homers, 100 RBI, and 100 runs in each of his six seasons—something no one else has ever done in even their first two. And as with all the great ones, his stats tell an incomplete story. "The best thing about Albert in a very long list of great things is that he plays the game to win," says La Russa. "That's what I admire most. Nothing else is a close second."

Similarly, the manager has dubbed Rolen the best defensive third baseman he's ever seen. Once the sole unanimous choice for an "All-Hustle Team" in an ESPN poll of executives and scouts, the five-time All-Star's ample run production is just a bonus.

In 2001, just two years after being a mere 13th-round draft pick, Albert Pujols was the Cards' first rookie position player in 52 years to make the All-Star Team. He is the only hitter ever to clear at least 30 fences in each of his first seven seasons.

Above: Jim Edmonds arguably should be the center fielder on a mythical Cardinals all-time defensive team. Offensively there is no comparison; Edmonds averaged 35 homers in his first six seasons with the team.

Left: Scott Rolen was in the prime of his career when he was acquired from the Phillies at the 2002 trading deadline. The seven-time Gold Glove winner is the finest defensive third baseman the team has ever had.

October Heartaches

Cardinals fans, like Susan Sarandon's character in *Bull Durham*, "worship at the church of baseball." For an entire decade, beginning in 1996, they were left standing at the altar.

The heroics, and heartaches, commenced with the installation of Tony La Russa as manager. Following years of wheel-spinning under Joe Torre, a seasoned group of veterans bonded under La Russa in 1996 to win the NL Central and sweep the Padres in the NLDS. With a three-games-to-one lead over the Braves, the forecast for a return to the World Series was bright. Then … fade to black. The Cards were outscored 32–1 over the next three contests.

Not even Mark McGwire's pyrotechnics could light the way until 2000, when the club danced to another division crown. Now entirely refashioned as a slugging (but somewhat sluggish) juggernaut, the Redbirds again navigated the NLDS unscathed only to be eliminated in the next round.

No team was hotter than the Cardinals at the end of 2001…until the playoffs, when the wild card "cinderellas" were ousted on the final pitch of the division series by Arizona. An emotional 2002 campaign saw the Cardinals sail into the NLCS. "It was almost like there was a plan for us," La Russa reflected. The best-laid ones, however, went awry in a five-game upset at the hands of the San Francisco Giants, again on a walk-off hit.

In both 2004 and 2005, St. Louis posted baseball's best record but left unfinished business. First swept by the underdog Red Sox in the 2004 World Series, they were upset once more the next season, this time by Houston in the NLCS. The Cardinals were bridesmaids again—but this time, they caught the bouquet.

The Cardinals took a three-games-to-one lead in the 1996 NL Division Series against the Braves before imploding. This Game 6 overthrow to first baseman John Mabry was emblematic of the mortifying collapse.

Jeff Suppan was an unheralded thinking-man's pitcher whose second-half valor carried the 2006 Cards to the promised land. Suppan compiled a 2.39 ERA in his last 15 outings and was MVP of the NLCS after allowing just one run in two starts.

Best Swept Team in Baseball

Baseball teaches that, on any given day, a weak-hitting batter can beat a pitcher with no-hit stuff or a nervous rookie can subdue the league's leading hitter…but karma is an invincible adversary. So no matter how much better the 2004 Cardinals were "on paper," no matter that their 105 wins represented their best showing in 60 years, theirs was a collision course with another team's destiny that could end no way but badly.

An argument could be made that this was the franchise's most balanced team ever. The Redbirds scored more and allowed fewer runs than any club in the NL; only two hit more homers; just one stole more bases. The middle of the order (Albert Pujols, Scott Rolen, and Jim Edmonds) averaged .316-41-119. There was one 20–20 man (Reggie Sanders), four 15-game winners, and a closer in Jason Isringhausen whose 47 saves tied a team record.

St. Louis showed heart, too, by pulling out Games 6 and 7 of the NLCS against Houston. But their World Series opponent was more than a team; it was a phenomenon. The Boston Red Sox, fresh off an ALCS miracle against the Yankees in which they were the first team ever to win a postseason series after trailing 3–0, were stalking the championship that had eluded them since 1918. The "Curse of the Bambino," it seemed, had been exorcised.

The Cards proved to be nothing but a trifling impediment to Boston's providence. Not only were they swept, but they were barely competitive in any game. The starting pitchers' ERA was 9.35, and the Edmonds/Rolen/Sanders segment of the lineup card went 1-for-39.

"It's an outstanding club, one of the neatest clubs to be around in 27 years of managing," Tony La Russa reflected dutifully. But the players were embarrassed and the fans were stunned. Lamented Edmonds, "We didn't even give them a chance to cheer."

After winning 105 games in the 2004 regular season, just one shy of the franchise record, the Cardinals beat Los Angeles and the Houston Astros in the NL playoffs to advance to the World Series for the first time in 17 years. They would play the Boston Red Sox.

Like Jeff Suppan at third base, the Cardinals were caught napping in the 2004 World Series, a mere pebble to be trodden on the Red Sox's road to destiny. Though heavily favored, they never even held a lead in any game.

131

When Mark McGwire surpassed Roger Maris's season record of 61 homers on September 8, 1998, he didn't stop hitting the ball out of the ballpark. His two home runs against Montreal on the final day of the season gave him the new record of 70.

Collectors and dealers of a variety of merchandise tried to cash in on "McGwire Mania" after Mark McGwire's record home run season. His face and likeness appeared on a variety of products, including commemorative plates and bobblehead dolls.

Sluggers Sammy Sosa and Mark McGwire

ANOTHER ITEM OF MEMORABILIA THAT SHOWED UP AFTER MARK MCGWIRE'S RECORD-BREAKING 1998 SEASON WAS A LUNCH BOX WITH A SET OF 30 BASEBALL CARDS HIGHLIGHTING THE MOST IMPORTANT HOME RUNS OF HIS CAREER.

FANS' LINGERING RESENTMENT OF THE 1994 PLAYERS' STRIKE/LOCKOUT DOGGED MAJOR-LEAGUE BASEBALL FOR THREE YEARS UNTIL 1998, WHEN TWO HALLOWED BASEBALL RECORDS WERE REWRITTEN. CAL RIPKEN'S STREAK OF MOST CONSECUTIVE GAMES PLAYED ENDED IN SEPTEMBER. MEANWHILE, MARK MCGWIRE AND SAMMY SOSA WERE SLUGGING BALLS OUT OF BALLPARKS AT A DAZZLING PACE, BOTH EVENTUALLY EXCEEDING ROGER MARIS'S SINGLE-SEASON HOME RUN RECORD.

NOT ONLY WERE FANS IN ST. LOUIS EXCITED WHEN MARK MCGWIRE BROKE THE HOME RUN RECORD, HIS YEAR-LONG BATTLE WITH THE CUBS' SAMMY SOSA MADE HEADLINES AND NEW FANS ACROSS THE COUNTRY.

Kings of the Hill

It has been a very long time since the Cardinals farm system gave birth to a great pitcher. Matt Morris, easily their leading winner over the past quarter-century, comes closest. After being the *Sporting News* NL Rookie Pitcher of the Year in 1997, the Seton Hall product wrote off most of three seasons to arm miseries but made a stirring comeback. In 2001, his 22 wins were tops by a Redbird since Bob Gibson in 1970. Morris remained an anchor of a fluid rotation through 2005, making two All-Star teams in the process.

A 2002 free agent signing buried in newspaper agate eventually became a banner headline. Chris Carpenter was a former hotshot prospect who had only a 49–50 record and a ravaged shoulder to show for his career with the Toronto Blue Jays. Though Walt Jocketty knew the right-hander was at least a year away from throwing another pitch, the GM's prescience and patience were rewarded when Carpenter—honed by ace pitching coach Dave Duncan—became the league's best starter from 2004 to 2006. His 51–18 ledger included a Cy Young campaign in 2005, when the Cardinals won 17 of his starts in a row. "It's just been a privilege to watch this kind of excellence," gushed Tony La Russa.

Most of the other starters in this era were simply keep-you-in-the-game types, which was just fine considering the quality of the relief pitchers that Cardinals managers could run out there. Beginning with Bruce Sutter's arrival in 1981, the Cardinals have amassed more saves than any team in the NL. Sutter passed the mantle to Todd Worrell, who handed off to Lee Smith (40-save average from 1990 to 1993), followed by Tom Henke (36 in 1995), and Dennis Eckersley (66 in 1996–1997). Another injury reclamation project, Jason Isringhausen, turned up in 2002, and he's since become the franchise's all-time saves leader.

Chris Carpenter's three-year run as staff ace included 2005, when he was positively Gibson-esque, reeling off 22 consecutive quality starts as the Cardinals won the last 17 games he went to the mound. His elbow surgery in 2007 derailed the team's title defense.

Injuries—a common theme for Cards starters in the past decade—may have separated Matt Morris from true greatness, but he was always a bulldog. In 2001, he set a team record with 15 home victories.

The "New Busch"

Cards fans may long remember the penultimate game of the 2005 season, but the final match—despite its historical significance—is best forgotten.

Just 48 hours after an exhilarating Albert Pujols three-run, ninth-inning homer in Houston kept the Cardinals viable in the NLCS, the team returned to St. Louis to bid adieu to Busch Memorial Stadium. It was a fleeting farewell. The anticlimactic elimination game ended 40 years of baseball there. Three weeks later, with semi-completed portions of the third Busch iteration standing as sentinels in the background, demolition began.

Whereas the architecture of the previous edifice merely evoked the Gateway Arch, the new $365 million facility imparted a majestic view of the renowned landmark in center field, with the St. Louis skyline brightening the panorama. Striking a discriminating equilibrium of the classic and the contemporary, Busch Stadium was conceived as both a shrine to the grand tradition of the franchise and a threshold to its future.

On April 10, 2006, the future began with a 6–4 win over the Milwaukee Brewers. By October, the ring of plaques outside commemorating the 100 Greatest Moments in Cardinals History required revision, as "New Busch" became the fourth stadium to host a World Series winner in its first year of operation. Unless another such spectacle intervenes, the stadium's next big confab will be the 2009 All-Star Game.

After 40 seasons in Busch Stadium, the Cardinals moved to a new Busch Stadium in 2006. They made the season a memorable one by becoming the first team since the Cincinnati Reds in 1970 to play in a World Series the same year they moved into a new stadium.

It was as if the ghosts of past success simply wafted across the parking lot as the demolition of "Old Busch" took place in the shadow of "New Busch" during the winter of 2005.

135

83 Wins and a World Title!

Tim McCarver, Cardinals catcher-turned-broadcaster, likes to say, "Baseball is a game of redeeming features." In 2006, the Cardinals were a bunch acutely in need of redemption. On six occasions in the preceding decade they had reached the postseason—several times as the team to beat—only to be rebuffed. The two most recent clubs were 100-game winners, one obliterated in the World Series, the next expelled by an inferior team from their own division.

One hundred games in, it seemed St. Louis (58–42) was in control of an unimposing NL Central. Then they dropped 36 of their last 61, suffering a seven-game and an eight-game losing streak while Houston closed 23–13 and made up eight games in as many late-September days. The Cards hung on but stumbled into the playoffs at a tepid 83–78. Beyond Albert Pujols's spectacular showing (.331-49-137), the offense was spotty. Outside of Chris Carpenter (15–8), the staff ERA was 4.81. Closer Jason Isringhausen was out with a hip injury, and Scott Rolen and Jim Edmonds were hurting.

And suddenly it all meant nothing.

Carpenter and Jeff Weaver (a midseason reinforcement) pitched magnificently in a four-game defeat of the Padres in the division series. In the NLCS against the heavily favored Mets, it was Jeff Suppan's turn to shine. After firing eight shutout innings and hitting a homer in Game 3, he handed a 1–1 Game 7 to the bullpen. Light-hitting catcher Yadier Molina laced a two-run

The Cardinals earned their revenge from 1968 by defeating the Tigers to win the 2006 World Series. A ticket to Game 4 gave fans a chance to see their Redbirds edge the Tigers 5–4 at Busch Stadium.

In a scene replicated for the tenth time—four more than any other NL franchise—the Cardinals reveled after the final out of a World Series championship. None in the modern era had fewer regular-season wins (83) than the 2007 edition, but neither did any NL club have more heart.

Diminutive David Eckstein, himself the poster child of baseball overachievement, is the author of an inspirational autobiography for children. Tony La Russa has called his shortstop "the engine, the personality, and in many ways, the identity of our team."

Most of the 2006 world champs signed this hot item.

cut by the Red Sox before he ever reached "The Show."

"You know," appraised the manager, "in this organization, until you win a World Series, you're not really part of 'The Club.' Now this team is part of 'The Club.'" Ten Cardinals teams are now members—more than any other franchise in the National League. The last was the unlikeliest to gain admittance; no other league champion in modern MLB annals has had a worse regular-season record.

"This city deserves it," said Edmonds. "It's a big sports city, and when you play in this city, you feel the whole city. You don't just feel it in the clubhouse. You feel the whole city behind you."

Win or lose. But mostly win.

homer in the ninth and ad hoc closer Adam Wainwright picked up a wobbly save to send St. Louis to the World Series against the Detroit Tigers. As underdogs, of course.

Whatever kismet had clotted itself into the Cardinals spikes was not about to dislodge now. Undistinguished freshman Anthony Reyes outdueled AL Rookie of the Year Justin Verlander in the opener. The Tigers evened it up, but Carpenter was formidable in a 5–0 Game 3 win. The fourth meeting was a gut-check on a wet Busch surface, the Cards plating the winning run in the eighth on an outfielder's slip, a wild pitch, and a single by David Eckstein.

The next night, the club remunerated its loyal legions for 24 years of sometimes impatient patience with a 4–2 clincher. Poetically, the World Series MVP was another overachiever, 5'6" shortstop/leadoff catalyst David Eckstein (called "the toughest guy I've ever seen in a uniform" by Tony La Russa), a former college walk-on who once had been

Eckstein ripped three doubles and a single in Game 4, then added two hits and two RBI in the Game 5 clincher. He gave the yellow Corvette he won as the 2006 World Series MVP to his brother because he couldn't drive a stick.

ST. LOUIS POST-DISPATCH

SATURDAY | OCTOBER 28, 2006 | FOUNDED BY JOSEPH PULITZER IN 1878 | STLTODAY.COM | 50¢

YES!

Laurie Skrivan | Post-Dispatch

CARDINALS WIN THEIR 10TH WORLD SERIES CHAMPIONSHIP • VICTORY PARADE SET FOR SUNDAY

CLOSER ADAM WAINWRIGHT AND CATCHER YADIER MOLINA HUG AFTER THE REDBIRDS CLAIM THE 2006 BASEBALL CROWN.

THE CARDINALS ACQUIRED JIM EDMONDS, DISPLAYED IN THIS MINIATURE STATUE, FROM THE ANAHEIM ANGELS IN A SPRING TRAINING TRADE IN 2000. HE BECAME ONE OF THE BEST DEFENSIVE CENTER FIELDERS IN FRANCHISE HISTORY, WINNING SIX CONSECUTIVE GOLD GLOVES.

ROOKIE PITCHER BUD SMITH EARNED HIS PLACE IN THE RECORD BOOK WITH HIS NO-HITTER AT SAN DIEGO ON SEPTEMBER 3, 2001. HE WON JUST SIX OTHER GAMES IN HIS SHORT TWO YEARS IN THE MAJORS, AND THE NO-HITTER WAS HIS ONLY SHUTOUT AND ONLY COMPLETE GAME.

THE CARDINALS ACQUIRED SCOTT ROLEN IN A TRADE WITH THE PHILLIES IN 2002. HE ENJOYED HIS BEST SEASON IN ST. LOUIS IN 2004, WHEN HE HIT .314 WITH 34 HOMERS AND 124 RBI. HE ALSO WON HIS THIRD CONSECUTIVE GOLD GLOVE AS A MEMBER OF THE CARDINALS.

THIS ALBERT PUJOLS BOBBLEHEAD DOLL IS A FAN FAVORITE. PUJOLS BURST ONTO THE MAJOR-LEAGUE BASEBALL SCENE IN 2001. HE WAS A UNANIMOUS CHOICE AS THE NL ROOKIE OF THE YEAR. HE BECAME JUST THE FOURTH ROOKIE IN HISTORY TO HIT .300 WITH 30 OR MORE HOMERS, 100 OR MORE RBI, AND 100 OR MORE RUNS SCORED.

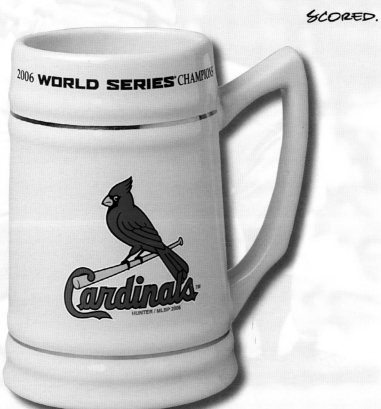

THE CARDINALS DID NOT ENJOY AS MUCH SUCCESS IN THE 2006 REGULAR SEASON AS THEY DID IN PAST SEASONS, BUT THEY WON WHEN IT COUNTED, WINNING THE NL PENNANT OVER THE METS AND DEFEATING DETROIT TO WIN THEIR FIRST WORLD SERIES TITLE SINCE 1982.

CHAPTER EIGHT

LEADERS AND LEGENDS

Team History

Team Names

St. Louis Brown Stockings/
   Browns (1882–1898)
St. Louis Perfectos (1899)
St. Louis Cardinals
   (1900–present)

World Series Winning Clubs (10)

1926, 1931, 1934, 1942, 1944,
1946, 1964, 1967, 1982, 2006

Pennant Winning Clubs (17)

1926, 1928, 1930, 1931, 1934,
1942, 1943, 1944, 1946, 1964,
1967, 1968, 1982, 1985, 1987,
2004, 2006

American Association Pennants (4)

1885, 1886, 1887, 1888

Division Winning Clubs (10)

1982, National League East
1985, National League East
1987, National League East
1996, National League Central
2000, National League Central
2001, National League Central
2002, National League Central
2004, National League Central
2005, National League Central
2006, National League Central

Playoff Wild Card Clubs

2001, National League Central
(tied for first with Houston
   but was appointed as the
   Wild Card)

Ballparks

Sportsman's Park (1882–1892)
Robison Field (1893–1920)
Sportsman's Park (1920–1966)
Busch Memorial Stadium
   (1966–2005)
Busch Stadium
   (2006–present)

Busch Stadium

Hall of Fame Members

Players elected with Cardinals logo on plaque

Lou Brock, LF (1964–1979)
Dizzy Dean, P (1930, 1932–1937)
Bob Gibson, P (1959–1975)
Stan Musial, LF/1B (1941–1944,
   1946–1963)
Red Schoendienst, 2B
   (1945–1956, 1961–1963),
   Manager (1965–1976, 1980,
   1990)
Enos Slaughter, RF (1938–1942,
   1946–1953)
Ozzie Smith, SS (1982–1996)
Bruce Sutter, P (1981–1984)

Players elected with Cardinals as their primary team

Jim Bottomley, 1B (1922–1932)
Frankie Frisch, 2B (1927–1937)
Chick Hafey, LF (1924–1931)
Jesse Haines, P (1920–1937)
Rogers Hornsby, 2B (1915–1926,
   1933)
Joe Medwick, LF (1932–1940,
   1947–1948)
Johnny Mize, 1B (1936–1941)

Bob Gibson

Retired Uniform Numbers

Ken Boyer—14
Lou Brock—20
Jack Buck—no number
Gussie Busch—85
Dizzy Dean—17
Bob Gibson—45
Rogers Hornsby—no number
Stan Musial—6
Jackie Robinson—42*
Red Schoendienst—2
Enos Slaughter—9
Ozzie Smith—1
Bruce Sutter—42

* Retired by all major-league clubs

Award Winners

National League

Triple Crown Winners

1922—Rogers Hornsby
1925—Rogers Hornsby
1937—Joe Medwick

Most Valuable Player

1925—Rogers Hornsby
1926—Bob O'Farrell
1928—Jim Bottomley
1931—Frankie Frisch
1934—Dizzy Dean
1937—Joe Medwick
1942—Mort Cooper
1943—Stan Musial
1944—Marty Marion
1946—Stan Musial (2)
1948—Stan Musial (3)
1964—Ken Boyer
1967—Orlando Cepeda
1968—Bob Gibson
1971—Joe Torre
1979—Keith Hernandez
1985—Willie McGee
2005—Albert Pujols

Cy Young Award

1968—Bob Gibson
1970—Bob Gibson (2)
2005—Chris Carpenter

Rookie of the Year

1954—Wally Moon
1955—Bill Virdon
1974—Bake McBride
1985—Vince Coleman
1986—Todd Worrell
2001—Albert Pujols

Manager of the Year

1985—Whitey Herzog
2002—Tony La Russa

Gold Glove

1958—Ken Boyer, 3B
1959—Ken Boyer, 3B
1960—Bill White, 1B
1960—Ken Boyer, 3B
1961—Ken Boyer, 3B
1961—Bill White, 1B
1962—Bobby Shantz, P
1962—Bill White, 1B
1963—Bobby Shantz, P
1963—Bill White, 1B
1963—Ken Boyer, 3B
1963—Curt Flood, OF
1964—Bill White, 1B
1964—Curt Flood, OF
1965—Bob Gibson, P
1965—Bill White, 1B
1965—Curt Flood, OF
1966—Bob Gibson, P
1966—Curt Flood, OF
1967—Bob Gibson, P
1967—Curt Flood, OF
1968—Bob Gibson, P
1968—Dal Maxvill, SS
1968—Curt Flood, OF
1969—Bob Gibson, P
1969—Curt Flood, OF
1970—Bob Gibson, P
1971—Bob Gibson, P
1972—Bob Gibson, P
1973—Bob Gibson, P
1975—Ken Reitz, 3B
1978—Keith Hernandez, 1B
1979—Keith Hernandez, 1B
1980—Keith Hernandez, 1B
1981—Keith Hernandez, 1B
1982—Ozzie Smith, SS
1982—Keith Hernandez, 1B
1983—Willie McGee, OF
1983—Ozzie Smith, SS
1984—Ozzie Smith, SS
1984—Joaquin Andujar, P
1985—Ozzie Smith, SS
1985—Willie McGee, OF
1986—Ozzie Smith, SS
1986—Willie McGee, OF
1987—Ozzie Smith, SS
1987—Terry Pendleton, 3B
1988—Ozzie Smith, SS
1989—Ozzie Smith, SS
1989—Terry Pendleton, 3B
1990—Ozzie Smith, SS
1991—Tom Pagnozzi, C
1991—Ozzie Smith, SS
1992—Tom Pagnozzi, C
1992—Ozzie Smith, SS
1994—Tom Pagnozzi, C
2000—Mike Matheny, C
2000—Jim Edmonds, OF
2001—Fernando Vina, 2B
2001—Jim Edmonds, OF
2002—Fernando Vina, 2B
2002—Scott Rolen, 3B
2002—Edgar Renteria, SS
2002—Jim Edmonds, OF
2003—Mike Matheny, C

1908 Glove

2003—Edgar Renteria, SS
2003—Scott Rolen, 3B
2003—Jim Edmonds, OF
2004—Scott Rolen, 3B
2004—Mike Matheny, C
2004—Jim Edmonds, OF
2005—Jim Edmonds, OF
2006—Albert Pujols, 1B
2006—Scott Rolen, 3B

Silver Slugger

1980—Bob Forsch, P
1980—Ted Simmons, C
1980—George Hendrick, OF
1980—Garry Templeton, SS
1980—Keith Hernandez, 1B
1983—George Hendrick, 1B
1985—Willie McGee, OF
1985—Jack Clark, 1B
1987—Bob Forsch, P
1987—Jack Clark, 1B
1987—Ozzie Smith, SS
1998—Mark McGwire, 1B
2000—Edgar Renteria, SS

2001—Albert Pujols, 3B
2002—Scott Rolen, 3B
2002—Edgar Renteria, SS
2003—Albert Pujols, OF
2003—Edgar Renteria, SS
2004—Jim Edmonds, OF
2004—Albert Pujols, 1B
2005—Jason Marquis, P

Batting Records

National League Leaders

Batting

1901—Jesse Burkett, .382
1920—Rogers Hornsby, .370
1921—Rogers Hornsby, .397
1922—Rogers Hornsby, .401
1923—Rogers Hornsby, .384
1924—Rogers Hornsby, .424
1925—Rogers Hornsby, .403
1931—Chick Hafey, .349
1937—Joe Medwick, .374
1939—Johnny Mize, .349
1943—Stan Musial, .357
1946—Stan Musial, .365
1948—Stan Musial, .376
1950—Stan Musial, .346
1951—Stan Musial, .355
1952—Stan Musial, .336
1957—Stan Musial, .351
1971—Joe Torre, .363
1979—Keith Hernandez, .344
1985—Willie McGee, .353

1990—Willie McGee, .335
2003—Albert Pujols, .359

Home Runs

1922—Rogers Hornsby, 42
1925—Rogers Hornsby, 39
1928—Jim Bottomley, 31
1934—Rip Collins, 35
1937—Joe Medwick, 31
1939—Johnny Mize, 28
1940—Johnny Mize, 43
1998—Mark McGwire, 70
1999—Mark McGwire, 65

Runs Batted In

1920—Rogers Hornsby, 94
1921—Rogers Hornsby, 126
1922—Rogers Hornsby, 152
1925—Rogers Hornsby, 143
1926—Jim Bottomley, 120

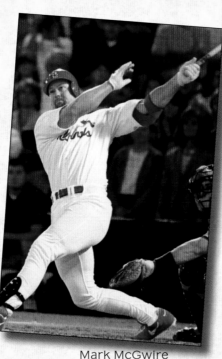
Mark McGwire

1928—Jim Bottomley, 136
1936—Joe Medwick, 138
1937—Joe Medwick, 154
1938—Joe Medwick, 122
1940—Johnny Mize, 137
1946—Enos Slaughter, 130
1948—Stan Musial, 131
1956—Stan Musial, 109
1964—Ken Boyer, 119
1967—Orlando Cepeda, 111
1971—Joe Torre, 137
1999—Mark McGwire, 147

Career Team Batting Leaders (Top 10)

Average

Rogers Hornsby—.359
Johnny Mize—.336
Joe Medwick—.335
Albert Pujols—.332
Stan Musial—.331
Chick Hafey—.326
Jim Bottomley—.325
Frankie Frisch—.312
George Watkins—.309
Joe Torre—.308

Home Runs

Stan Musial—475
Albert Pujols—282
Ken Boyer—255
Jim Edmonds—241
Ray Lankford—228
Mark McGwire—220
Rogers Hornsby—193
Jim Bottomley—181

Stan Musial

Ted Simmons—172
Johnny Mize—158

Runs Batted In

Stan Musial—1,951
Enos Slaughter—1,148
Jim Bottomley—1,105
Rogers Hornsby—1,072
Ken Boyer—1,001
Ted Simmons—929
Albert Pujols—861
Ray Lankford—829
Joe Medwick—823
Lou Brock—814

Stolen Bases

Lou Brock—888
Vince Coleman—549
Ozzie Smith—433
Willie McGee—301
Ray Lankford—250
Jack Smith—203
Frankie Frisch—195
Miller Huggins—174
Lonnie Smith—173
Tom Herr—152

Pitching Records

National League Leaders (* = tie)

Victories

1934—Dizzy Dean, 30
1935—Dizzy Dean, 28
1942—Mort Cooper, 22
1946—Howie Pollet, 21
1970—Bob Gibson, 23*
1984—Joaquin Andujar, 20
2001—Matt Morris, 22*

Earned Run Average (ERA)

1914—Bill Doak, 1.72
1921—Bill Doak, 2.58
1942—Mort Cooper, 1.77
1943—Howie Pollet, 1.75
1946—Howie Pollet, 2.10
1948—Harry Brecheen, 2.24
1968—Bob Gibson, 1.12
1976—John Denny, 2.52
1988—Joe Magrane, 2.18

Strikeouts

1906—Fred Beebe, 171
1930—Bill Hallahan, 177
1931—Bill Hallahan, 159
1932—Dizzy Dean, 191
1933—Dizzy Dean, 199
1934—Dizzy Dean, 195
1935—Dizzy Dean, 190
1948—Harry Brecheen, 149
1958—Sam Jones, 225
1968—Bob Gibson, 268
1989—Jose DeLeon, 201

Career Team Pitching Leaders (Top 10)

Victories

Bob Gibson—251
Jesse Haines—210
Bob Forsch—163
Bill Sherdel—153
Bill Doak—145
Dizzy Dean—134
Harry Brecheen—127
Mort Cooper—105
Slim Sallee—105
Max Lanier—101
Larry Jackson—101
Matt Morris—101

Earned Run Average (ERA)

John Tudor—2.52
Slim Sallee—2.67
Jack Taylor—2.67
Johnny Lush—2.74
Red Ames—2.74
Mort Cooper—2.77
Fred Beebe—2.79
Max Lanier—2.84

1942 World Series Ticket

Harry Brecheen—2.91
Bob Gibson—2.91

Strikeouts

Bob Gibson—3,117
Dizzy Dean—1,087
Bob Forsch—1,079
Matt Morris—986
Jesse Haines—979
Steve Carlton—951
Bill Doak—938
Larry Jackson—899
Harry Brecheen—857
Vinegar Bend Mizell—789

Shoutouts

Bob Gibson—56
Bill Doak—32
Mort Cooper—28
Harry Brecheen—25
Jesse Haines—24
Dizzy Dean—23
Max Lanier—20
Howie Pollet—20
Bob Forsch—19
Ernie Broglio—18

Saves

Jason Isringhausen—173
Lee Smith—160
Todd Worrell—129
Bruce Sutter—127
Dennis Eckersley—66
Lindy McDaniel—64
Joe Hoerner—60
Al Brazle—60
Al Hrabosky—59
Dave Veres—48

1964 Pennant

St. Louis Cardinal Hall of Fame Lineup

Catcher
Roger Bresnahan 1909–1912

First Base
Orlando Cepeda 1966–1968

Second Base
Rogers Hornsby 1915–1926, 1933

Third Base
John McGraw 1900

Shortstop
Ozzie Smith 1982–1996

Outfield
Stan Musial 1941–1944, 1946–1963

Outfield
Lou Brock 1964–1979

Outfield
Enos Slaughter 1938–1942, 1946–1953

Pitcher
Bob Gibson 1959–1975

INDEX